TRAVESTY
A True Crime Story

The Du Pont Kidnap Case
And the LaRouche Railroad

TRAVESTY
A True Crime Story

The Du Pont Kidnap Case
And the LaRouche Railroad

by An EIR Investigative Team

Executive Intelligence Review
Washington, D.C.
1993

Cover design: Alan Yue
Cover photograph: Philip Ulanowsky
Back cover photograph: Stuart Lewis
ISBN: 0-943235-09-X

Copyright © 1993 by Executive Intelligence Review

Library of Congress Catalogue number: 93-70623

Printed in the U.S.A.

For information, contact the publisher
Executive Intelligence Review
P.O. Box 17390
Washington, D.C. 20041-0390
EIB 93-003

CONTENTS

v

Illustrations follow pages 57, 103, 141

ACKNOWLEDGEMENTS

WHAT FOLLOWS IS A TRUE STORY. The dialogue in this book is composed of the actual words of the conspirators, captured without their knowledge by FBI tape recorders. The recordings were made by FBI undercover operative Doug Poppa, as well as court-ordered wiretaps. Other material for this book is taken from FBI witness reports and other documents made public during the trial of *U.S. v. Smith, et al.*, Criminal Number 92-420-A in the Eastern District of Virginia. Trial testimony is taken from the official transcripts of the case.

THIS BOOK WAS PUT TOGETHER by an investigative team headed by Bruce Director and Warren A.J. Hamerman, that included Gail Billington, Barbara Boyd, George Canning, Mary Jane Freeman, Fredric Henderson, Sanford Roberts and Susan Ulanowsky. Many others also provided information and corroborated facts, whose contributions did much to enrich the story.

FOREWORD

This book tells the story of how dirty the United States government is, and the depth and extent of corruption in the courts and the U.S. Department of Justice.

Four years ago, on January 27, 1989, Lyndon LaRouche was thrown in prison, where he still sits today, a political prisoner, an innocent man and a victim of gross and outrageous government misconduct carried out in concert with private hate groups.

On May 4, 1988, an intended federal court frame-up of Mr. LaRouche had ended in a mistrial in Boston, Massachusetts. The government's prosecutorial team had steadfastly denied any and all entanglements with private citizens and intelligence community "secret government" political enemies of LaRouche; they also denied the existence of any exculpatory evidence in this regard. Yet, the federal judge on the case, Robert E. Keeton, formally cited the government's "systemic and institutional prosecutorial misconduct" in ordering the mistrial. One of the jurors told the press (*Boston Herald*, May 5, 1988) that the jury was polled and believed that "some of the government's people caused the problem, adding that the evidence showed that people working on behalf of the government 'may have been involved in some of this fraud to discredit the campaign.' "[1]

Only five months after the Boston case ended in the stench of government misconduct, on October 14, 1988, the federal government again indicted LaRouche, this time in the infamous "rocket docket" of the Eastern District of Virginia in Alexandria. Chief Judge Albert V. Bryan Jr., a specialist in supervising the highest-level cases involving national security and state secrets, ran the railroad. Before trial, the prosecution team again steadfastly denied any "concert of action" with private elements and sanctimoniously denied the existence of exculpatory evidence of government misconduct. Then, before the railroad trial began, Judge Bryan shut down the defense that had been prepared, and elminated all evidence of government misconduct. After a fixed trial fraught with irregularities and injustices outside international "fair trial standards," LaRouche and six of his associates were convicted.[1]

The government lied, suppressed evidence and suborned perjury in Boston and Alexandria. The courts allowed the prosecutors to cover up their own abuses.[1]

For three years, while LaRouche was falsely imprisoned, his lawyers and investigators amassed unprecedented amounts of evidence of the outrageous government misconduct which had been used in his prosecution. On January 22, 1992, LaRouche filed a monumental motion in federal court, a 2255/Rule 33 motion, seeking to vacate his sentence because his conviction and detention were unlawful. The principal ground for LaRouche's immediate release was that massive amounts of newly obtained evidence prove that "the prosecution conducted and participated in a conspiracy and concerted action with others to illegally and wrongfully convict him and his associates by engaging in outrageous misconduct, including financial warfare." The motion was backed by six volumes of evidence of government misconduct newly obtained after the trial.[2]

Then on September 30, 1992, five men were arrested for a violent felony crime: conspiring to kidnap Lewis du Pont Smith, an associate of LaRouche. The conspirators included Don Moore, a former deputy in the Loudoun County, Virginia Sheriff's Department, who had been at the center of government misconduct against LaRouche since 1985; professional kidnapper and "deprogrammer" Galen Kelly; Kelly's lawyer, Robert "Biker Bob" Point; Lewis Smith's father, E. Newbold Smith, who bankrolled the conspiracy; and Tony Russo, an ex-cop who had been involved in previous kidnappings with Kelly.

This is a play with more than one Iago.

Don Moore was the assigned Lee Harvey Oswald of a seven-year-long anti-LaRouche conspiracy. He was the designated fall guy, the lower-level "gopher," the arms and legs of an apparatus which had engaged in years of illegal investigations against LaRouche and his associates. Don Moore, a man who brags of his close association to Iran-Contra figure Ollie North, was characterized by his own lawyer at trial as "the G. Gordon Liddy of Loudoun County." Gordon Liddy was the intelligence community's Watergate criminal who specialized in "black bag" illegal break-ins and other dirty tricks. His philosophy, like Iran-Contra's Oliver North and Richard Secord, as well as that of Don Moore and his co-defendants, was that he was one of the chosen elite who operated above the law for a "secret government" where the ends justify the means.

As you will learn in this book, Moore's personal and philosophical association with Ollie North and the secret government was at the center of a Grenada-style, 400-man paramilitary assault against American political leader Lyndon LaRouche, just 50 minutes outside of Washington in the rolling hills of Northern Virginia's

Hunt Country. The invasion force into the town of Leesburg on October 6, 1986 involved helicopters, an armored
personnel carrier, SWAT teams, and a private, quasi-
military police backup force called ARGUS (Armored Response Group U.S.). The official pretext for the raid by an
assortment of state, national, and local law enforcement
agencies was to seize truckloads of financial documents
for criminal investigations. The actual, underlying intent
of the secret government elements of the raid was to stage
an incident in which Lyndon LaRouche would have been
assassinated in a shootout.

Another prominent conspirator in what has become
known as the Kidnappers, Inc. trial was professional kidnapper and brainwasher Galen Kelly. Kelly is not just
another thug. He is part of an international apparatus of
Israeli, American, and British secret intelligence communities' "wetworks" capability. "Wetworks" is an intelligence community term for assassinations and physical
violence against targetted people. In the kidnappers' conspiracy, Kelly and Moore discussed various "wetwork"
scenarios involving Israeli musclemen from the notorious
Lubavitcher sect, motorcycle gangs and paramilitary ex-
intelligence community operatives. Kelly is on the board
of JINSA, the Jewish Institute for National Security Affairs, a liaison group between Israeli and American military establishments that is suspected of having been at
the center of the Jonathan Jay Pollard spy ring. Kelly is
also the security henchman and a paid employee of the
Cult Awareness Network (CAN).

The Kidnappers, Inc. trial evidence included more
than 60 hours of consensually monitored surveillance
tapes and court-ordered wiretaps of conversations among
the conspirators, in which they bragged of illegal conspir-

atorial activity with government investigators and prosecutors against LaRouche, going back to 1985. In this
book, you will be able to read for yourself large sections
of the transcripts which were made available to the public.
It is estimated that 94-95 percent of the tapes that were
recorded, were never allowed into the public record by
the government—before, during or after the trial.

The evidence exposed the central illegal role which
two hate-mongering and anti-First Amendment organiza-
tions had in the government misconduct against
LaRouche. These organizations are the Anti-Defamation
League of B'nai B'rith[3] (ADL) and the Cult Awareness
Network (CAN).

The Kidnappers, Inc. trial was held in the same Alexandria courthouse where LaRouche's railroad had occurred four years earlier, almost to the day. The lead
defense lawyer for the kidnappers was none other than
John Markham, the former prosecutor of LaRouche in
the Boston and Alexandria trials. A key defense witness
who committed blatant perjury on the witness stand was
Virginia Assistant Attorney General John Russell, the
prosecutor of LaRouche's associates in the Virginia state
trials. The legal adviser to defendant Don Moore at a
pretrial hearing was former LaRouche co-prosecutor
Mark Rasch. Present in the courtroom during the trial,
giving assistance or support to the kidnappers, were the
ADL's Mira Lansky Boland, ex-NBC-TV reporter Pat
Lynch, and other key members of the concert of action
against LaRouche.

We had hoped that the full evil truth would come to
the light of day. We hoped the case of Kidnappers, Inc.
would bring a just verdict. It did not. We hoped that the
truth would come to the attention of the public. It did not.

Therefore, we are publishing this book to bring the case before the court of world history.

Dear reader, it is said that the United States is a democracy concerned with fair play and justice; but herein is the story of one of the most corrupt dictatorships in history. Look out your window. Injustice is rampant in the land.

Let those who believe they are above the law not maintain their fleeting illusions.

We are thoroughly confident of divine justice.

"Blessed are they which are persecuted for righteousness' sake: for theirs is the kingdom of heaven."
—The Sermon on the Mount, Matthew 5:10

Notes

1. For this and all references to the judicial frame-up and railroading of LaRouche, see the extensive documentation in the book *Railroad; U.S.A. v. Lyndon LaRouche, et al.* Commission to Investigate Human Rights Violations, 1989, Washington, D.C.

2. For the documentation of the 2255 *habeas corpus* motion filed by Lyndon LaRouche, and of the illegal government/private "concert of action," see the pamphlet *LaRouche Launches Major Legal Effort for Freedom*. Commission to Investigate Human Rights Violations, 1992, Washington, D.C.

3. See *The Ugly Truth About the ADL*. Executive Intelligence Review, 1992, Washington, D.C.

PROLOGUE

This story begins on the night of May 5, 1992. It is near downtown Washington, D.C., around 11:00 p.m. A young, professional woman is walking to her car, which is parked in the loading dock entrance to the American Institute of Architecture building off 18th St. N.W. The woman, leaving her part-time job, is carrying several bags. As usual, the street is quiet, and slightly foreboding, like all streets of northwest Washington that time of night. She approaches her red Dodge hatchback, and she glances across the street. There is a white van with some maroon markings parked opposite her car. Giving the van only a passing thought, the woman opens the back of her car and begins putting some of her packages in the rear.

Suddenly, she is aware of two white men dressed in jungle fatigues walking toward her. One of the men is tall and slim with dark, wiry hair and a moustache. The other is shorter and stockier, sporting a multi-colored grey, white and brown beard. The stocky man starts to speak as if to ask the woman a question. The woman runs to get into the car. The two men rush her. Thinking she's about to be murdered or robbed, she screams, panic-stricken. The men grab her, throwing her on the hood of the car. The tall man grabs her legs, spreading them wide apart, pressing his crotch against hers. The stocky man grabs her upper body, twisting her arm and banging her against the hood of the car. She thrashes desperately, sure she's about to be raped. Trying to free herself, she screams for help at the top of her lungs.

There is pain as the stocky man squeezes her wrist and twists her arm. The tall man grabs her ankles. The men drag her across the street and force her, through the side door, into the van. She struggles desperately, grabbing the sides of the van, hanging on to her bags. Her right leg is caught under the van. The men are too strong. Her resistance fails. They force her inside. The tall man jumps into the driver's seat, while the stocky man gets in the back with her. The door slams. The van speeds away, heading for Virginia.

The abduction takes only a few minutes. The young woman's ordeal is just beginning.

The inside of the van is bare, with only a blue carpet on the floor. In the passenger seat is a pot-bellied, middle-aged woman with bright orange hair, and a puffy, pock-marked face. She has dark circles under her eyes. In the very back, blocking the rear door, is a younger, fatter woman with brown hair. Both women are members of the Lubavitcher cult, described by their critics as a group of Orthodox Jews involved in organized crime.

As the van pulls away from the curb, the stocky man and the fat woman push the young woman toward the back. They order her to sit near the left wheel well.

"Get your hands off me. I'll sit down by myself," the young woman protests, trying to regain some dignity.

As she touches the floor, she jumps back up, complaining the floor is wet.

"It's not wet," the stocky man insists, pushing the young woman back into the puddle of water on the floor. When the young woman refuses to sit in the puddle, the stocky man grabs her and pushes her to the other side of the van, ordering her to keep her hands still.

"What's your name?" the young woman asks the stocky man, who is now sitting opposite her.

"Kelly," he answers.

"Kelly who?"

"Galen Kelly."

◆ ◆ ◆

Though the name means nothing to her, Galen Kelly is the most notorious professional kidnapper/deprogrammer in the United States, with close ties to Israeli intelligence and criminal and terrorist circles. Kelly has kidnapped countless people over the years, picking up substantial fees for his services. Most of his clients are parents who believe their children are involved in cults. For a fee, Kelly kidnaps their children, to hold them against their will, and subject them to what he calls "deprogramming," which is more akin to brainwashing and torture than psychotherapy. Most of Kelly's business comes as referrals from the Cult Awareness Network, or CAN, as it's called, a national clearinghouse and referral service for kidnappers-for-hire like Kelly.

"Where are we going? How long till we get there?" the bewildered young woman asks. Kelly doesn't answer. He only tells her they're going to meet someone who wants to talk to her. And all she has to do is listen.

"How things go depends on you," Kelly warns her. "If you cooperate, it will go okay. If you don't, we can do things to you to make you cooperate. We have a whole slew of techniques from drugs to other various methods that would force you to cooperate. The situation could be made progressively adverse. It depends on you. By cooperation, I don't mean just saying yes, I mean really somehow engaging."

This last remark baffles the frightened young woman. Who would want to see me? she wonders. Kelly gives her the impression it's her mother, but this makes no sense to her.

As the van drives on, the young woman sees, through a tiny corner of the van's window, the lights of the city growing dimmer, and the road getting increasingly dark. They cross the Capital Beltway, and head further into the Virginia countryside.

The woman is becoming increasingly miserable. It's damp and cold in the van. On top of that, she's starting to get her period and she has no tampons. She complains to Kelly that she's becoming a bloody mess, but he says there's nothing he can do. The fat woman in the back of the van says she'll give her some tampons when they get to where they're going.

Their destination is Carradoc Hall, a motel on the outskirts of Leesburg, Virginia, about 45 miles northwest of Washington, D.C. Leesburg is the county seat of Loudoun County, located in Virginia's Hunt Country, where the wealthy living on Middleburg estates raise horses, ride in fox hunts, and otherwise enjoy the good life. Waiting at the motel is Kelly's accomplice, Donald Leigh Moore, Jr., a 45-year-old, recently fired Loudoun County Deputy Sheriff who has gone into the kidnapping business with Kelly. With Moore is an older woman who has hired Kelly and Moore to kidnap her daughter, because she believes her daughter is having a lesbian relationship. The mother wants her daughter "deprogrammed" away from her lesbian lover.

The older woman is nervous. She has paid thousands of dollars to Kelly for this moment. Her excitement heightens as the van pulls into the parking lot.

When the van stops, the pot-bellied woman with orange hair leaves the van and goes into the motel, while Kelly, the tall man, the fatter woman and the kidnap victim wait in the van.

"Here she comes," announces the tall man. "She looks nervous." The older woman climbs into the passenger seat and turns around, looking at the young woman sitting in the back. A flustered look comes over her face.

The older woman hesitates. "That's not her," she says finally.

"It's not B—? I didn't think so," Kelly responds.

"S—?" The older woman asks the victim.

"No, it's not S—," Kelly interjects, "It's D—."

"I don't know D—. I know S—," the older woman says, staring in disbelief at the young woman, who is thinking the older woman is actually her roommate's mother.

"Stand up," commands the older woman, still refusing to believe that Kelly kidnapped the wrong woman. The young woman refuses.

The older woman gets out of the van, as panic sets in among the kidnappers. After a few moments, Kelly regains his cool. As an experienced kidnapper, he's been in tight situations before, and he's always gotten out of them. He can get out of this one, too, he thinks.

Turning to the young woman, he tells her he was paid substantial amounts of money to kidnap the older woman's daughter. She now has to help him get the right woman, implying this is a condition of her release. One of the fat Lubavitcher women says, "Let me get my knitting needles. I can make her talk."

The young woman is in no mood to cooperate. She's cold and damp and bloody. She asks Kelly to let her get some tampons. Kelly lets the fat woman in the back of the van leave. About five minutes later, she returns with five or six tampons. The young woman begs to be let out of the van to go to the bathroom, but Kelly won't let her. Instead, the van pulls out of the parking lot. Kelly tells the woman they're taking her back.

Kelly now has two problems to solve. He still wants to find the right woman to kidnap, but he also has to keep this woman from going to the police.

He tells her he will make things difficult for her if she doesn't help arrange a meeting between Kelly and her roommate. Kelly threatens to get her fired from her job by telling lies about her to her boss. He repeatedly tells her he will make her very sorry if she tells anybody about anything that happened to her. He tells her he will take "bloody revenge" against her.

The young woman refuses to cooperate. Kelly continues to pressure her, repeating his threats.

As the van nears Washington, D.C. the driver seems confused and lost. Concerned that they might try to kidnap her roommate that night, the young woman asks to be let out at any downtown hotel. Instead, the van goes to 18th St., near where she left her car. At a stoplight, the woman is told to get out of the van as the door is opened, and she is pushed out. She has the bags she was carrying when she was kidnapped, but her thermos is missing. She runs back to the van and asks for her thermos. As the van pulls off, Kelly throws the thermos out the window. The FBI would later find Kelly's fingerprint on the thermos.

Frightened, the woman goes back to her car, looking around nervously for signs of Kelly. Her jacket is still on the street. She fishes her keys out of her jacket pocket, gets in her car and drives home. It's 3:20 in the morning.

Still angry and in a state of shock, the young woman calls her roommate at work, tells her what happened, and warns her to be careful. Her roommate decides to leave town before dawn. At 4:00 a.m., the kidnap victim calls the D.C. police, and is directed to the Sex Squad. At 8:00 a.m. she calls her lawyer. She's tired and wants to sleep, but her lawyer tells her to make a report right away, which she does. After going through her belongings, she notices that Kelly has stolen $175 from her.

Meanwhile, Kelly and the Lubavitchers have sped away into the night. Kelly is confident his threats were effective enough to keep the young woman from going to the authorities. Nevertheless, as a precaution, Kelly will simply hide out for a while until the incident blows over. He'll just have to put his other clients on temporary hold.

◆ ◆ ◆

Don Moore figures he's at less risk, since the victim never saw him. He remains in Loudoun County, where he's in the middle of a public controversy with the local Sheriff, John Isom. Moore, who had once seemed to be Isom's fair-haired boy, has been fired by Isom, and Moore is now laying the groundwork to run for Sheriff as a Republican against Democrat Isom, who is reportedly being investigated by the FBI for unspecified irregularities in his department.

Since his firing, Moore has been keeping busy. He's had other work to do, on another project he's doing with Kelly. But with Kelly in hiding, Moore has to carry on by himself.

After waiting only a month after the botched kidnapping in May, Moore decides to enlist another out-of-work Sheriff's Deputy named Doug Poppa. Moore and Poppa had both been fired by Isom, but for different reasons: Moore for rifling files to which he had been denied access, and Poppa for exposing that the Sheriff's Department had withheld evidence in a shooting case.

On June 26, 1992, Doug Poppa is in his Leesburg apartment talking with another Sheriff's Deputy, Pete Becerra, when Moore calls, saying he wants to come over to talk about how Poppa can make some money. A short while later, while Becerra is still there, Moore arrives.

"I may have a job for you doing surveillance," Moore says.

He explains that he's working for the Cult Awareness Network (CAN) and has been hired to "snatch" and "deprogram" a son of the Du Pont family. The plan, Moore says, is to have a woman lure the younger Du Pont to a hotel, drug him, and then take him to his father's yacht 60 miles off the coast where he would be "deprogrammed." In less than five minutes, Moore leaves.

Poppa looks at Becerra: "Moore is crazy." He doesn't say what else he and Becerra are both thinking—that Moore is planning a federal crime: kidnapping.

After Becerra leaves, Poppa calls the FBI, trying to reach Special Agent Scott Sutherland. He knows Sutherland is working on an FBI investigation of Sheriff Isom, Poppa's former boss. The FBI agent he reaches asks Poppa to try and tape record any further conversations he has with Moore. He's told he'll be reimbursed for any expenses. Poppa agrees.

Unbeknownst to Poppa, Becerra does almost the same thing. Becerra has heard Moore say crazy things before, but nothing *this* crazy. However, Becerra, still employed by the Sheriff's Department, proceeds more cautiously. After thinking about it for a few days, he tells his supervisor what happened. He then reports it to the FBI. As far as Becerra is concerned, the matter is now out of his hands.

◆ ◆ ◆

What follows is the story of the planning and organizing of the kidnapping of Lewis du Pont Smith, an heir to the Du Pont chemical fortune, and an associate of Lyndon LaRouche. The story was captured on Doug Poppa's secret tape recorder. Confronted with this evidence, federal government prosecutors were forced to bring charges against what has become known as Kidnappers, Inc.

You, dear reader, will not only see the plot unfold, but you will see how some of the most powerful forces in the U.S. establishment who were ultimately behind this conspiracy to kidnap, were the same forces who were also behind the railroading and imprisonment of their political enemy, Lyndon LaRouche. These are the people who have so perverted America's judicial system that innocent people are railroaded to prison, while the guilty can get off, scot-free.

1 | A Lot of Heavy Players

Finally, four days later, at 10:00 p.m. on June 30, 1992, Doug Poppa calls Don Moore.

"How ya doing?" Moore says, answering the phone.

"Well, I'm hanging in there. Hey, did you hear that the county might go to—they're starting to look into going to a county police force," Poppa starts the conversation.

"I was hearing about something about that—Barton had something about going to a charter," Moore says, referring to the County Board of Supervisors Chairman George Barton, a crony of Moore. "And that is probably, at least, well—it's at least a couple of years away from anywhere," Moore says.

"Right," Poppa responds.

"I'm not certain they can get it done before the next election. Let's put it that way," Moore offers his opinion.

"Right."

"But, frankly, I've never thought of fighting that idea. As a matter of fact, I think that if I ran, I would say I would completely concur with any studies that were done." Moore is thinking that he will run for Sheriff of

Loudoun County, Virginia, against the present Sheriff, John Isom.

"Right," Poppa says.

The two men continue discussing the dominant story in county politics, the case of William Douglas Carter. Carter is a Middleburg man convicted in 1988 of shooting his ex-wife. His conviction had been overturned in February 1992, largely due to testimony by Poppa that the Sheriff's Department and Commonwealth's Attorney's office had withheld exculpatory evidence. Carter is facing a retrial beginning in July.

"How's your thing going?" Poppa asks, trying to change the subject. "Are you doing anything or—" Before he can finish, Moore interrupts.

"Yeah, as a matter of fact. I went up to Philadelphia and at some point here we need to get together. I'm working on a project and if there—I may be able to dovetail you in on this thing. It involves a cult. It involves operating, doing some surveillance up in the Philadelphia area."

"Right—on that Jewish thing you were talking about?" Poppa asks.

"It involves that to a certain extent. It's more complicated than that," Moore says.

"Right."

"It's typical of things I get into. A lot of very heavy players are in this thing. So, mistakes can not be made," Moore states.

◆ ◆ ◆

Poppa would soon be introduced to some of these heavy players. Moore has been dealing with them for years. In the fall of 1985, Loudoun Sheriff Isom had appointed

Moore to head up an investigation of Lyndon LaRouche. LaRouche and some associates of his had moved to Loudoun County, Virginia. Moore's position gave him special authority that meant he didn't have to answer to anyone, not even to his immediate superiors in the Sheriff's Department.

The local weekly newspaper, the *Loudoun Times-Mirror,* had printed a letter from Moore in its May 21, 1992 issue, in which Moore gave this account of his role in the LaRouche investigation:

"Isom was dragged into the LaRouche investigation, kicking and screaming, by me. He tried to shut down the investigation on several occasions. . . . When a deputy came to me and told me in late 1985 that the Criminal Investigations Division (CID) of the department was corrupt and would 'screw up' or 'sell me out,' I subsequently refused to allow any portion of the LaRouche investigation to be included in departmental records or to have CID personnel involved in any way with the investigation. To my knowledge, it is the only investigation in the history of the department handled in that fashion."

For the next seven years, Moore conducted illegal dirty tricks against LaRouche and his associates in coordination with LaRouche's powerful enemies. The dirty tricks were the kinds of things Moore and his Vietnam tentmate and LaRouche adversary, Oliver North, did in Southeast Asia, and the kinds of tricks North had later coordinated out of the National Security Council. Moore had served in a Civic Affairs unit in Vietnam; and like his former tentmate Ollie North, he had never psychologically recovered from his experiences. Yet, this psychologically unbalanced man wore a badge, carried a gun, and operated under the authority of state and federal officials.

To Moore, Leesburg was a strategic hamlet, and LaRouche and his associates were infiltrators from the North.

Moore also worked closely with the Anti-Defamation League of B'nai B'rith (ADL), an organization that was much more than a group ostensibly protecting Jewish civil liberties; its prominent connections include British Freemasonry, organized crime, and international drug trafficking. In the late 1970s, when LaRouche's political movement launched an all-out war on drugs, the ADL went all out to protect the drug profits of the international banks, and went to war against LaRouche. Around that time, Canon Edward West, of the kookish Episcopal Cathedral of St. John the Divine in New York City, declared on behalf of LaRouche's enemies that "we will not deal directly with him. We will have our Jewish friends in the ADL deal with Mr. LaRouche and his organization." These were the same "Jewish friends" with whom Moore and Kelly worked.

♦ ♦ ♦

On the evening of July 1, Moore comes over unexpectedly to Poppa's apartment. Poppa is outside talking to his neighbor, and does not have time to set up his tape recorder. He and Moore go into Poppa's apartment to talk.

Moore tells Poppa that the kidnapping targets he has been talking about are Lewis du Pont Smith and Smith's wife, Andrea Diano Smith. He says the kidnapping is being sponsored by Edgar Newbold Smith, Lewis's father.

♦ ♦ ♦

E. Newbold Smith is an internationally renowned yachts-man, from a prominent Philadelphia Main Line family with blood relations to the British royal family—Princess Diana of Wales is a sixth cousin. Newbold Smith's marriage to Lewis's mother, Margaret du Pont (known as Peggy), united two of the most prominent families in the Social Register. Smith summed up his personal credo as: tackle low; the U.S. Marine Corps is invincible; the Church of England has Holy Rightness; and never marry a Catholic. As each of his three sons reached maturity, Smith passed on this credo, expecting them to live by it. Lewis was the only son to reject it.

The elder Smith, enraged by his son's support for the establishment's enemy Lyndon LaRouche, joined forces with the ADL, CAN, and anyone else he could find, in an effort to destroy LaRouche and LaRouche's movement. He considered Lewis "brainwashed," and was determined to break him. He hired the kidnapper/deprogrammer Galen Kelly to do the job.

◆ ◆ ◆

The plan, Moore says, is to drug the younger Smith and cart him off to be "deprogrammed." The deprogramming is to be done by Galen Kelly with assistance from the Lubavitchers, the Orthodox Jewish cult. Moore makes no mention of the botched Washington, D.C. kidnapping he and Kelly had done in May.

Moore says he needs Poppa to do surveillance now, but that later on, he might be involved in what's known as "wetworks"—intelligence community lingo for physical attacks on individuals.

If "wetworks" become involved, Moore says, they could make up to $1 million, but, at that point Poppa will have the option to opt in or opt out. If he chooses to opt in to "wetworks," Moore says, Poppa can name his price.

Poppa doesn't wait long before recontacting the FBI to report this latest discussion with Moore. When the FBI agents hear that Moore mentioned the name of Galen Kelly, they take Poppa's report very seriously. By now, they have received a report of the D.C. kidnapping, and have opened an investigation into it. FBI agents in New York are also investigating Kelly and some Lubavitchers in connection with a 1991 kidnapping there.

On July 6, the FBI asks Poppa to cooperate with their investigation as an undercover agent. Poppa agrees.

♦ ♦ ♦

Undercover work is not new to Poppa. For the last decade, he had conducted undercover drug operations for the Loudoun County Sheriff's office, and had gained a reputation as a courageous and trustworthy law enforcement officer. It wasn't until early 1992 that Poppa ran into trouble with his superiors. It was then that he came forward with information that Sheriff John Isom and Loudoun County Commonwealth's Attorney William Burch had withheld exculpatory information in the Carter shooting case. Poppa had stuck to his story, despite extreme pressure, including a demotion from narcotics investigator to process server; when Poppa talked to the press about the Carter case, Isom canned him.

While Poppa's revelations had caused a firestorm in Loudoun County, the Sheriff had other problems. Reports had surfaced of widespread corruption among high officials in the Sheriff's office. A scandal arose over the Sheriff's involvement in a private paramilitary group called Armored Response Group United States (ARGUS). An

FBI investigation was initiated. According to press reports, the FBI was looking into misuse of evidence and financial irregularities. In April 1992, FBI agents raided the Sheriff's Department, seizing boxes of records to take before a grand jury.

It was also in this context that Isom fired Don Moore in March, reportedly for rummaging through the Sheriff's garbage.

♦ ♦ ♦

On the evening of July 6, with FBI agent Scott Salter in the room, Poppa places a call to Moore, asking Moore if he has any work for him.

"I won't know until tomorrow. I have to get approval to use both of us here, and if I can do that, then you're in and we'll work something out. I imagine you can get anywhere from $80 to $100 a day or something like that, but you'll be living free, anyway. Then, who knows how things will improve from there," Moore responds.

2 | I'm Working for CAN

At 9:34 on the morning of July 7, Moore calls Poppa, but no one answers, so he leaves a message that everything's go. At 11:25 a.m., in the presence of two FBI agents, Poppa returns the call.

"We can go late this evening or early tomorrow morning up to Philadelphia," Moore says. "What it'll be is $100 a day and then probably a half of a day going up and a half of a day coming back, food on premises; you're living in a mansion and there is a maid that will cook for us. It'll probably be something in the neighborhood of $400 for four days."

"I don't have a problem leaving tonight," Poppa responds.

Moore explains that they'll be doing surveillance of offices and getting license plate numbers of cars. Moore also says there may be additional work for Poppa.

"There's another LaRouche case popping from CAN," Moore says.

"What's CAN?" Poppa asks.

"CAN is the Cult Awareness Network," Moore answers. "It's a consortium I work for—you're not going to understand it the first time I tell it to you, okay?"

"Right."

"Just imagine there are groups within groups within groups. They are for every purpose anti-cult, okay?" Moore says.

"Uh huh," Poppa replies.

"Against them, usually family members and people like that, you are trying to get their kids out, okay?" Moore continues, "So, there's Moonies and anti-Moonies. There are LaRouchies and anti-LaRouchies, okay? All the antis got together and formed CAN. Within those organizations you got small organizations that still focus on the particular cult they are against, all right? They send money in. It's kinda like the United Way, in the sense that each one collects money and they send some money into CAN and CAN acts as an umbrella organization."

"Right," Poppa responds.

"Right now I am doing some work for CAN under its umbrella against LaRouche people, and then I'm also doing work for Newbold, who funds the LaRouche anti-group, okay?" Moore goes on, "What I want to do is kinda introduce you into the scenario here."

"You sure nobody is actually setting us up on anything, like with this guy you're talking about, Kelly—" Poppa probes.

"No, no, no, no, no."

"You know this guy, right?" Poppa asks.

"No, no, no, no. This ain't—this is nothing. Believe me, I have known these folks longer than I have known Isom, and on the way up, I will explain it further. But I know this outfit better than—these guys are long-time players," Moore says reassuringly.

Moore tells Poppa he'll pick him up after 6:00 p.m. "Just pack a bag for three days, bring your passport and whatever time we leave here, you'll have at least 20 or 30 minutes warning. Well, I'll call you before I come."

◆ ◆ ◆

The Cult Awareness Network for which Moore has been working was originally called the Citizens Freedom Foundation. It was founded in 1974 by Henrietta Crampton and a small group of advocates of "deprogramming," a euphemism for making someone change their beliefs by force, otherwise known as Korean or Chinese Communist "brainwashing."

A prime force behind the formation of CFF was Ted Patrick, who has been convicted numerous times for violent crimes. Patrick wrote in his book *Let Our Children Go!* that deprogramming involves "kidnapping at the very least, quite often assault and battery, almost invariably conspiracy to commit a crime and illegal restraint."

Since its founding, CAN has changed its name, gotten more prominent sponsors, and broadened its affiliations. But it has always remained the same: a clearinghouse and referral service for kidnappers for hire.

As Bucknell University religion professor Larry Shin aptly told the *Philadelphia Inquirer* in 1992, deprogramming is "the most destructive of the legacies of the great American cult scare. . . . CAN is much closer to a destructive cult than most of the groups they attack."

Since the mid-1980s, CAN has functioned as the most active of a throng of so-called anti-cult organizations which sprang from the ravages of the counterculture. Such groups as the Jewish Community Relations Council's (JCRC) Task Force on Missionaries and Cults, the

American Family Foundation, the International Cult Education Project and the Interfaith Coalition of Concern About Cults, all share interlocking boards of directors and funding. They give each other awards and share referrals. Through these associations, CAN has enjoyed the support and protection of powerful elements of the eastern liberal financial establishment.

CAN claims to maintain files on over a thousand organizations which it deems to be "destructive cults," and they distribute hate literature against many of them. But if an inquirer asks for more information about a particular organization, CAN will eagerly refer the inquirer to its "experts" on the particular organization. The "experts" are deprogrammers, who for a fee will arrange a kidnapping/deprogramming. A typical "deprogramming" fee is $20,000.

Estimates are that CAN maintains a network of 20 to 25 full-time deprogrammers and 30 or so part-time deprogrammers. Each full-time deprogrammer lands approximately 25 deprogramming jobs per year, making a conservative estimate of over 500 deprogrammings per year. Of those deprogrammings, 25 percent involve outright kidnapping. The rest involve detaining the victim against his or her will. It has been reported that at the 1992 CAN conference in Los Angeles, a CAN deprogrammer claimed that over 2,000 deprogrammings occurred in the United States in the last year.

Occasionally, deprogrammers are arrested. Most frequently, they plead guilty to lesser charges and spend little or no time in jail. Often, they go scot-free.

At CAN's national conferences and local meetings, family members interested in having someone kidnapped or deprogrammed can meet professionals like Galen Kelly, whom they can hire.

3 One Black Bag Job After Another

"**S**peak to me! Okay, I hope we're on the air. It's 20:11 hours on Tuesday the 7th. I believe Don Moore's just rolling up outside right now." Doug Poppa speaks into his hidden microphone, as he prepares to leave for Philadelphia on the evening of July 7. The FBI's chase team is ready to follow.

. As they get in the car, Moore takes a roll of hundred dollar bills from his pocket, peels off four and gives them to Poppa. Once in the car, Poppa asks Moore about the man they're working for.

"This guy, Newbold—uh, reminds me of some big black guy with a bald head."

"No, no, no, no, no, white guy in his seventies, sounds like a hundred years old," Moore interrupts, sounding a bit bemused at Poppa's disrespect for someone of Newbold Smith's superior station.

"What are these, rich snobby type of people, or what?" Poppa asks.

"Well, uh, they're not snobby," Moore answers matter-of-factly. "He's very plain-spoken, but he's an ex-Marine, too. I mean, he served, and his father was a very famous Marine colonel."

Actually, Newbold Smith never served in the Marines. He was a graduate of the U.S. Naval Academy, where he was an all-American football player. But his military service was spent in a desk job at the Philadelphia Navy Yard, where he was not far away from his family's mansion.

Yet Moore, as an ex-Marine, would allow himself a moment to feel a certain fraternity with Newbold Smith, even though they were social classes apart.

Quickly catching himself, Moore adds, "But he's very well aware of class distinction. And the whole family is too. And I mean they know, I mean, the Du Ponts were raised as Du Ponts."

Moore's reverence for Smith's social standing is intense, but his insight is nevertheless accurate. "You understand, I think the reason he's trying to get his son back has less to do with the fact that he's his son, than the fact that he's a Du Pont and he's gone astray."

◆ ◆ ◆

Moore, driving his 1980 gray Oldsmobile sedan, doesn't head straight for Philadelphia. First he stops at Dulles Airport, where he sends a Federal Express package to Cynthia Kisser, the executive director of CAN. Kisser is planning to file a libel suit against *New Federalist,* a newspaper published by LaRouche's associates, and she has asked Moore for help.

The *New Federalist* had published an article exposing CAN's associations with kidnappers, brainwashers and perverts. The article revealed, among other things, that CAN's former president, an Episcopal priest named Rev. Michael Rokos, had been forced to resign as head of CAN when the *Baltimore Sun* published a report that Rokos had been arrested in the early 1980s for soliciting a male undercover police officer for illicit sex. According to an affidavit signed by the arresting officer, James G. Wyatt, Rokos solicited him, saying, "I want you to tie me up, put clothespins on my nipples and make me suck your dick."

Kisser knows the suit is a nuisance suit intended only to harass the LaRouche movement.

After stopping at McDonald's for something to eat, the two men head for the printing company where Moore's wife works. He goes in for a brief moment, comes out and gets back in the car.

It's now almost 9:00 p.m., and the men are finally getting on the road to Philadelphia. As they drive north on U.S. 15 towards Frederick, Maryland, the periods of silence are broken by talk of the scandals in the Sheriff's Department, old police stories, and Moore's plans to run for Sheriff. Moore does most of the talking. Poppa and his tape recorder do the listening.

Soon, the talk turns to Moore's role in the LaRouche prosecutions, which include not only LaRouche, but a number of his associates, most of them located in Virginia.

Moore says the Internal Revenue Service "did not have the Social Security numbers for 90 percent of the LaRouche people."

"No shit," Poppa responds.

"They did not have it for anybody, and I did. Want to know how I got it? Voter registration," Moore brags.

"Really?"

"When you vote—when you register to vote, you sign a card with your name and signature across the bottom, says where you live, your Social Security number, your date of birth, and your last place of register. I've got burned copies of every voting card they ever submitted. A gal from voting registration helped me do it. Illegal as shit." Moore relishes his chicanery. "When the time came, I had Lyndon LaRouche's voting registration card, because he registered to vote. These guys were screwing— I said, wait a minute. There's going to be an election in Leesburg and I'm going to register to vote. They registered tons of people in two days," Moore brags.

"Right."

"I got all the cards. I was right in there—you know, they didn't know me from Adam. Burning copies left and right, just like part of the registrar. 'Okay, fine, sir, you step right over here, make a copy for our files,' and you know, followed right up. One for me, one for you. So, if you ever want to find a Social Security number in Virginia, and in a lot of other places, too, um, go to the voting records, because most of those records are public," Moore offers.

He talks of putting them into a special computer that Newbold Smith had purchased for him. He talks of other dirty tricks, such as how he recruited the daughter of a local postmistress to get information from one of LaRouche's security guards, whom she was dating.

He talks at length about his theory of cults. Then, worn out from talking, Moore wants to stop for a drink.

"I'm dying of thirst. You okay?" he asks Poppa.

"Yep."

"Okay. Being large, fat, old and slow, I drink a lot of liquids."

Moore doesn't stop talking as they pull into a Roy Rogers drive-through. He orders two large lemonades and they pull around to the cashier.

"Why didn't you just get some undercover guys, give

them a false identity, and let them go in there and fuck it from the inside?" asks Poppa.

"Part of the problem we had—and again you wouldn't believe this, but it happens to be true. The FBI truly fucked with the LaRouche organization in, oh, what they called Cointelpro program."

"Right."

"Believe it or not, the LaRouchies are really not lying up to about 1980—let's say '81 or '82."

Moore hands the cashier $3.00 and gets back 45 cents in change. After carefully balancing the lemonades so they won't spill, Moore continues. "But anyway, we had—there's an FBI gal who I know quite well. She went under the name, I keep calling her Nicky Johnson, but I can't think of her real name now, because we always called her Nicky, just so she wouldn't blow her cover. Um, and she was getting some good shit out of Boston. All of a sudden Markham realized that—Markham was the prosecutor, John Markham—that—he started doing some work checking up on some of the FBI—three-year previous investigations. Holy shit! This is nothing but one, one black bag job after another on these guys."

◆ ◆ ◆

In fact, the FBI's illegal operations against LaRouche went on for much longer than three years. Under the infamous Cointelpro (Counter Intelligence Program), the FBI deployed agents provocateurs into the LaRouche movement for illegal purposes, including an attempted assassination of LaRouche. According to the FBI's own documents, in late 1973, the FBI was planning to help the Communist Party U.S.A. "eliminate" LaRouche. The plan was foiled when LaRouche publicly exposed the assassination plot.

Yet, FBI illegal operations against LaRouche continued. In 1975 LaRouche sued the FBI. The suit, known as *LaRouche v. Webster*, is still being litigated to this day. So far, the FBI has stonewalled on releasing crucial parts of its voluminous files on LaRouche. These files contain documents that prove a decades-long campaign by the U.S. government to wipe out the LaRouche political movement.

And now, new evidence has been made public that sheds more light on the motive behind the FBI's vendetta against LaRouche. According to a February 9, 1992, Public Broadcasting Service documentary on "Frontline," the late FBI Director J. Edgar Hoover was a gambler and homosexual who was blackmailed by the same elements of organized crime that run the ADL. Reportedly, organized crime boss Meyer Lansky possessed photographs of Hoover having homosexual sex, and used these photographs to blackmail Hoover. Mob figures also placed bets for Hoover and sponsored vacations for Hoover and his assistant, Clyde Tolson—who was also reportedly Hoover's lifelong homosexual lover.

Susan Rosensteil, the wife of Louis Rosensteil, a gangster who ran the Schenley's liquor company, reports in the TV documentary that she attended a party at the Plaza Hotel in New York City, at which J. Edgar Hoover was dressed up as a woman and was having sex with her husband and mob lawyer Roy Cohn. Cohn was a notorious homosexual, who died of AIDS.

Hoover protected these mob bosses, and in turn used the FBI as a "gestapo" against political figures the mob didn't control.

4 | They Want Him Out

When they reach Frederick, Maryland, Don Moore, still talking, heads east on Interstate 70 towards Baltimore, where he'll pick up Interstate 95 north towards Philadelphia. The conversation turns to the background of the man Moore and his fellow kidnappers have been hired to kidnap.

In 1985, Lewis du Pont Smith, then a history teacher at a Quaker high school outside Philadelphia, put up $212,000 of his own money to help finance the publication of the book *Dope, Inc.* The book, commissioned by Lyndon LaRouche, was a detailed exposé of how the Anglo-American banking establishment finances the international narcotics traffic. The first printing of *Dope, Inc.* in 1978 had set the ADL into motion against LaRouche.

By the mid-1980s, a second, expanded version, subtitled *Boston Brahmins and Soviet Commissars*, had been produced. The book not only attacked the very families associated with Lewis's parents, but it took special aim at the dope-dealing connections of the Canadian-based

Bronfman organized crime family of Seagram's whiskey fame.

This was a point of some sensitivity for the Du Ponts, since Edgar Bronfman had purchased a controlling interest in E.I. Du Pont de Nemours Company, and had installed Irving Shapiro as its president. Shapiro and Bronfman were both high officials and funders of the ADL.

♦ ♦ ♦

"So this guy gets in and gets fucked up—he's already fucked up before he gets in there, right? And what, they start stealing his money?" Doug Poppa asks, referring to Lewis Smith.

"Well, what happens next is the parents find out he's in the organization. They move rapidly to have him declared mentally incompetent. They've got a problem, because the trust was set up by the grandfather. It is what is called an irrevocable trust," Moore explains. "Which means that no matter what happens, the kid gets the money."

"Right. Whether they actually have him declared a mental incompetent—" Poppa interjects.

"Yes, and he is now. The story gets long and involved, and so, strap yourself in." Moore enjoys revealing the strange tale to Poppa, a neophyte to the LaRouche cases. "What happens next is, after they declare him mentally incompetent, the LaRouche people start using their lawyers to try to get him declared un-mentally incompetent."

"Right." Poppa is puzzling over the meaning of "un-mentally incompetent."

"Now, the judge up in Pennsylvania is a judge named Woods, sided with the family, basically, but what he said was, 'Okay, instead of having you fight his interests, I will appoint the Wilmington Trust Company to represent the trust as a separate entity from Lewis or the family.' "

"Right. Right," Poppa says.

"And they will take such actions as they deem necessary to protect the principal, which is to say the $6 million, and he can spend the income any way he wants to," Moore goes on.

"Right."

"So they won and they lost, all right? So he's got this income that comes from—the principal's still there. But the income, which is about, just under $20,000 a month, you know, he can do anything he wants with."

"Right," Poppa says.

"And, obviously, he's given it to them. Now, in the meantime, the LaRouchies try another tactic. They have a girl that he met. They bring her into the organization, and they try and get him to marry her," Moore spins his tale.

"She's a LaRouchie?" Poppa asks.

"She was a LaRouchie—well, she wasn't in the beginning, but she was later on. When she got married to him, she was a LaRouchie. They had met—he had talked to her about it, sort of brought her in, but in a way he didn't."

"Right."

"But basically, the idea here is to get him married. Well, he tries to get married in the United States, and nobody will marry him because he's mentally incompetent."

"Right," Poppa responds.

"There's a court order against him. Now they then go to Italy and get the dumb fuckin' Italians—excuse me, to go to, believe it or not, one of the Curia, underneath the Pope, one of the cardinals, and they say, 'Listen, this is a case of political repression against Catholics,' " Moore goes on.

"Right."

"Now, Newbold is an Episcopalian. Well, he doesn't—you know, he's got members of Catholics in his family anyway."

"Right."

"That's not what they tell this priest. They tell this priest, you know, he's a rich Episcopalian and he hates Catholics, and he had his son declared incompetent and they can't get married in the United States. Will you marry them in the Catholic Church in Italy? Now, the marriage is not recognized in the United States," Moore continues.

"Right," Poppa interjects.

"All right. But the LaRouchies come back and they do this big political thing, and if I recall what they—when Ronald Reagan ran the second time, one of the Republican challengers early on was a guy named Pierre du Pont, who was the governor of Delaware."

"That's right."

"And what happened was, Lewis would scream, 'Free my people,' de-da-da-da. You know, just become an embarrassment. Well, the family has never challenged the marriage, and they let him go on and live, but they've never given her a cent."

"Right."

"So he's living and married to this Adrian Dian—Andrea Diano."

◆ ◆ ◆

This part of Moore's story is not true. The Smith family bitterly opposed Lewis's marriage. After all, the fourth dictum of Newbold's creed was "never marry a Catholic." But Lewis wouldn't let his father's bigoted edict stymie his love for Andrea, so the couple, with the help of the Vatican, were married on December 14, 1986 by a Catholic priest, Don Dario Composta, in a ceremony in the Church of Santa Maria del Popolo in Rome, Italy. And, at the request of the groom, Lyndon LaRouche flew to Rome to be the best man.

Newbold Smith was incensed. He pressured the Catholic Church to block the wedding. Failing that, he went back before Pennsylvania Judge Lawrence Wood, who had declared Lewis incompetent, to have the marriage invalidated. For the next year, Lewis and Andrea battled to have their marriage legalized in the United States, while Newbold vilified his son's new wife. Andrea was accused of being a "seductress for LaRouche," and a victimizer of Newbold's supposedly mentally incompetent son. Newbold used his power and influence to have baseless criminal charges brought against Andrea in California, which were later dropped. The family even sought a guardian for the couple's unborn and yet-unconceived children. Finally, after a year and a half, Judge Wood validated the marriage.

◆ ◆ ◆

Poppa settles in for what is now becoming a long ride. The FBI chase team is following, and his tape recorder is running, so he doesn't miss the opportunity to glean as much information as possible from Moore. He learns that Newbold and Peggy Smith are in Maine at their summer home, and that Lewis's older brother Stockton, or Stocky, as he's called, is a former Navy fighter pilot who's now taken over the family's business and is plotting with his father against his brother. Stockton, an admirer of Oliver North, has maintained his connections to Naval Intelligence since he got out of the Navy. He is known as a detail man.

"What's the other guy do? The one we're interested in—Lewis," Poppa asks.

"Oh, Lewis, what he does, is he goes every day to the offices at Upper Darby and he helps them fundraise," Moore replies.

"Oh, but he has nothing to do with the family business?"

"No, he has nothing to do with the family business. He's on a trust," Moore reiterates. "You know, he was cut out of all that—"

"But he's totally away from the family. He's involved with LaRouche?" Poppa persists.

"That's exactly right."

Poppa tries to sum it all up. "So, thus far I got you as—all right, the Du Ponts are rich, they got all these business interests. Stockton is with the business. This guy is the outcast, so to say, declared him mentally incompetent. They're pissed because he married this woman and obviously his money is going to the dickhead LaRouches."

"You got it," Moore proclaims.

"They want him out."

"That's exactly right."

"My question is—" Poppa continues.

"How?" Moore interrupts.

"No, I mean, so they do. What's going to stop him from going back?"

Poppa's question brings Moore back around to the kidnapping plans and the subject of deprogramming.

"I brought some pretty big people out," Moore brags, referring to the LaRouche political movement. "But you got to have unlimited access, and frankly, unlimited time."

"Right."

♦ ♦ ♦

"Bringing people out," or deprogramming, a technique of brainwashing, has its roots in the CIA's mind-control experiments of the 1950s and '60s, code-named MK-Ultra. The theoretical guru of deprogramming is Yale psychiatrist Robert J. Lifton, whose book *Thought Reform and the Psychology of Totalism* is the bible of CAN's deprogrammers. Lifton marvelled at the ability of the Communist Chinese to use isolation, confession and threats of physical or psychological abuse to "re-educate" enemies of Mao Zedong's regime. Along with Dr. L. Jolyon West, Margaret Singer, Richard Ofshe, and other CIA-linked psychologists, CAN adopted these techniques, and made them into a lucrative business. This is the business that now employs Moore.

♦ ♦ ♦

"Now, Newbold's basically got me on salary. And I won't be doing the deprogramming. There's a guy named Galen Kelly—it's a name you should get to know, because Ga-len—Galen and I worked for probably, shit, I can't say,

well, ever since the beginning of LaRouche, since '85,"
Moore says.

"Right."

"Galen's got an interesting history. Very intelligent
guy, majored in psychology, became one of the first people to recognize that cults were dangerous, back in the
early '60s. Started doing what was very primitive deprogramming. Back in those days they used to just grab,
snatch people on the street, kidnap them, and deprogram
them. He got hauled in on a kidnapping beef, did not get
convicted, but it sort of changed his tenor. He went off to
do corporate security kinds of investigations."

"Right."

"Didn't like it. A lot of people would call him up, say,
'Save my son or daughter, save my son or daughter.' He's
nationally known as the guy to do that. Where Galen
and I fit together is Galen doesn't know dick about the
LaRouche organization."

"Right."

"Frankly, Doug, you're talking to the only guy who
does. It's one of those. It sounds funny, but it's one of
those things that, I've looked around—nobody knows
what I know."

"Right."

"So Galen and I joined forces on the LaRouche case
and he's been teaching about the other cults. I've been
teaching him about LaRouche. And we're very much co-
equals in this enterprise."

"Right."

"Galen apparently has had another kidnapping go
bad. He's on the lam. He's been out of the socket for about
three weeks now."

Moore is loosening up. He just keeps right on talking,

as if there's nothing wrong with a former law enforcement officer associating with criminals, or planning to carry out what he knows are criminal acts. Poppa lets him talk. But Moore's not yet ready to let Poppa in on everything. He conceals, for now, his own involvement in the Washington, D.C. kidnapping-gone-bad. In any case, Moore's not worried about breaking the law.

"There's one thing I forgot to tell you. Stocky, the guy who's chairman of the Board of Atlantic Airline—CIA."

"Oh, is he really?" Poppa asks in disbelief.

"Proprietary, it's like Air America."

"Right."

"Okay. That's the reason—if things get icky, that's going to be our out, because nobody will go after," Moore says.

◆ ◆ ◆

The CIA did have ties to at least one Du Pont family airline, the one called Summitt Aviation, which was founded in 1960 by Richard C. du Pont, Jr., a cousin of Lewis. Summitt Aviation had supplied planes to the CIA for use in supplying the Nicaraguan Contras, the operation coordinated from the National Security Council by Moore's former tentmate, Oliver North.

In the mid-1980s, LaRouche had blown the cover on North's operations, showing they were nothing more than a government-sanctioned gun- and drug-running network run by sections of the U.S. and Israeli intelligence communities. In response, North used his networks to go after LaRouche. LaRouche's trial in Boston in 1988 was scuttled because of government misconduct, after a May 1986 telegram surfaced from Richard Secord to North stating, "Our man here is gathering information to be used against LaRouche."

The "our man here" the telegram referred to was retired Master Sergeant John Cupp, an operative in North's operations to supply the Nicaraguan Contras. It was known that some persons contributing to causes associated with the LaRouche political movement, were also contributors to Ollie North's operations, and that North was trying to stop contributions from going to LaRouche-associated causes.

◆ ◆ ◆

With the kidnapping plans proceeding along, under the the protection of what Moore believes to be the CIA through Stockton Smith, he's confident of success. But there's still an unsolved problem: what to do with Andrea, Lewis's wife. The Smith family hates Andrea, and sees her as an impediment to the successful kidnapping and deprogramming of Lewis. Moore agrees.

"If he deprograms him, he gets him out, then he's out. All right. The problem we got is the girl is still in, he may have some love for the girl, I don't know. Both of them may have to come out," Moore explains.

"Right. She's a LaRouchie," Poppa says.

5 | Busting the Covey

The night is dragging on, but Doug Poppa still has a lot to learn. The plot to kidnap Lewis Smith isn't just beginning. It's actually been going on for quite some time. Newbold Smith has been plotting to kidnap his son for the last five or six years. Since he hired Galen Kelly, numerous attempts have been made.

In December of 1986, Kelly helped organize an attempt to kidnap Lewis Smith in Paris, France, after he and Andrea had gone to Europe to be married. Newbold Smith ordered the operation and his son, Stockton, worked out the details. Stocky had hired a private investigator named Chuck Wunder, of Mays Landing, New Jersey, to carry it out.

According to an itemization of expenses dated June 3, 1987 that was submitted to Stockton Smith, Wunder conferred numerous times with Galen Kelly before leaving the United States for France. Once in France, he surveilled Lewis and hired several French nationals to help.

When details of this kidnapping attempt were presented to Pennsylvania Judge Lawrence Wood, who was then presiding over the incompetency proceedings against Lewis, Wood issued a sealed restraining order preventing Newbold Smith from doing anything to impede Lewis's freedom of movement or liberty. Newbold wasn't going to let a court order stop him. He chose to ignore this one.

So, in the fall of 1991, Kelly hired a New Jersey waitress named Carol Hoffman to assist him. Hoffman is the daughter of a cop, and met Kelly through his attorney, Robert "Biker Bob" Point, of South Amboy, New Jersey.

"Now we had tried a deal with sending in this gal—let's put it this way, her morals could be had for the right amount of money, but she's not a pro," Don Moore tells Poppa without naming Hoffman.

In September 1991, Kelly, Point and another Kelly crony, Anthony Russo, had taken Hoffman to Upper Darby, Pennsylvania, where Lewis Smith was working at the offices of Eastern States Distributors, Inc. (ESDI), a non-profit company that distributed, throughout the mid-Atlantic states, political literature supporting the LaRouche political movement. Hoffman was paid $200 to surveill Lewis and join the health club where Lewis regularly exercised.

"With the idea of enticing him out, getting him to screw her a couple of times, creating an affair and then snatching him with the idea that he would be lending himself to his own abduction," says Moore, giving Poppa an abbreviated version of the plan.

"That still has some promise, but that has been put on the shelf for now. What we are looking at right now is what I'm calling 'Grenade the Chicken Coop' or 'Busting the Covey.' You'll hear that expression used," he says.

"What did you call it? Bust what?" Poppa asks, perplexed.

"Busting the covey. You've heard of a covey of quail?" Moore is speaking in his best Marine Corps tone.

"Right."

"Okay, if you've ever busted a covey, you run right into the middle and all the birds go—"

"They go flying, right," Poppa completes the sentence.

"Okay," Moore continues, "grenade the chicken coop, same idea. Okay, pluck, pluck, pluck, everybody goes. What I am trying to do is bust the covey up here."

Moore explains his plan. He says that ESDI is going to move their offices into the new house that Lewis and Andrea have just purchased in the well-to-do Chestnut Hill section of Philadelphia. His plan is to plant stories in the local papers and rile up the neighborhood against Lewis and Andrea.

"We'll call a press conference. 'The LaRouchies are now in your neighborhood,' " he says, and "we don't want the riff-raff around." It doesn't matter to Moore that Lewis and Andrea have no plans for their new home other than to live in it. He has another reason for spreading the story which he now divulges to Poppa.

"So anyway, we're going to bust the covey. Now, on the shelf, we're also going to have an—and I'm just telling you this, and it's not to be repeated—but at some point in time there will be an operation, that you will have nothing to do with."

"Right."

"That is called the A-team. It is also called wetwork. You hear the expression wetwork, you don't need to know about it, or the A-team, all right?"

"Right."

"That will be a group of Jewish guys who will just move in, do it."

"Right."

"Busting the covey may or may not cause this thing to happen. The death of LaRouche could cause it to happen—breakup in the organization," Moore declares.

♦ ♦ ♦

Moore had had plenty of experience with what he now called "busting the covey." Probably the most flagrant was in 1985, when he, along with the ADL and their assets in Loudoun County, Virginia, convinced citizens and the county government that a summer camp for children was actually a terrorist training center.

The camp, called Sweetwater Farm, was located in the foothills of the Blue Ridge Mountains in the northwestern part of Loudoun County, an area of rolling farmland near a high-security telecommunications relay station owned by AT&T.

The camp had been purchased by some friends of LaRouche who invited the children of LaRouche supporters from around the world to spend the summer, enjoying traditional summer camp activities such as hiking, swimming, and arts and crafts, as well as music, drama, cooking, drawing and painting, and science experiments. At first, the camp was well received.

Then Moore, with the help of Mira Lansky Boland, the Washington, D.C. fact-finding director of the ADL, Polly Girvin, an ADL-connected lawyer who apparently moved into Loudoun County just to agitate against the summer camp, pro-drug lawyer Philip Hirschkopf and a local eccentric, Frank Raflo, then chairman of the County

Board of Supervisors, set out to spread lying gossip throughout the county that the camp was a secret training ground for terrorists.

Wild stories appeared in the local newspaper, the *Loudoun Times-Mirror*, authored by reporter Bryan Chitwood, a notorious drunk. The stories accused LaRouche associates of conducting weapons training, mutilating animals, and making violent threats against local residents. A local group was formed, Defense Against LaRouche Fund (whose acronym was DARF), to spread the rumors and hysteria.

The hysteria reached such a fever pitch, that when the request for a special exception permit to operate the camp reached public hearing, a frenzied mob that had come to believe its own lies showed up to testify, and the county denied the permit to operate the camp. Months later, when a judge from another county was brought in to review the decision, he called the zoning board's action "just plain wrong."

Just such a use of Nazi-propagandist Joseph Goebbels' "big lie" technique was repeated on a national scale in the news media after two associates of LaRouche won state-wide Democratic primary elections in Illinois in March 1986. The intended result was to so ostracize LaRouche and anyone associated with him, that physical assaults and political frameups could be conducted with impunity.

◆ ◆ ◆

As they continue the drive to Philadelphia, Poppa keeps probing Moore. "This guy Kelly is out of this thing, right?" Poppa asks.

"Well, no. Kelly is out of it for now. And if he's back in, he won't be doing operational kinds of things."

"Right."

"His big thing is wetwork and deprogramming."

"Right."

"What we have decided to do, we've done on the other organizations, is I set up the plan. I come up with a plan, I set up the plan, I gather in the intelligence."

Moore continues, "I point out where the guy is, the houses, all the stuff. With that information, they go in. That way there's distinct breakoff. I can say, hey, I didn't know they were gonna kidnap him."

"Right," Poppa says.

"I'm just doing what they asked me to find out. I've found out, I've given a report and I've walked away."

"Right."

"And that's what we're gonna do."

"Right."

"So it gives, it gives Newbold plausible denial, gives me plausible denial, gives everybody plausible denial," Moore says, adding, "at the other end of it, they're gonna have a tough time busting up the Jews,"

"What do you mean the Jews, busting the Jews?" Poppa asks.

"Well, what I mean is if they ever caught any of them, these guys would not—"

"What are they, Mossad?" Poppa interrupts, referring to the Israeli intelligence agency that is comparable to the CIA.

"No, they're, there's a connection in there. But that's another thing. There's a second Jew who's called a Lubavitch."

"Luba who?"

"Lubavitch, Lubavitchers."

"Hasidic Jews?" Poppa was from Brooklyn, so he knew about the Hasidic Jews in New York.

"No, no, no, no, these guys, well, they are Orthodox, but they don't wear the curls and the flat hats and busbies and the whole nine yards. But they're a Jewish cult. These Jews believe that it is their religious mission to fight cults."

"Right."

"Capture of the mind. And so they capture people who are part of cults," Moore says.

"Then they take them off to Galen and he deprograms them," Moore finishes.

♦ ♦ ♦

Galen Kelly always used Lubavitchers or members of the terrorist Jewish Defense League as musclemen for his kidnappings. Kelly himself has long had a close relationship with Israeli intelligence. In 1986, Kelly was on the board of directors of the Jewish Institute for National Security Affairs (JINSA), an organization of high-ranking officials of the U.S. military establishment that functions as the liaison with the Israeli Defense Forces.

Officials of JINSA are suspected of being accomplices of Jonathan Pollard, the former U.S. naval analyst convicted of spying for Israel. When Kelly was on the board of JINSA, its advisory board included such luminaries as ADL officials Minnesota Sen. Rudy Boschwitz and Nathan Perlmutter; U.N. Ambassador Jeane Kirkpatrick; Eugene Rostow; retired Adm. Elmo Zumwalt; Bush HUD Secretary Jack Kemp; and political analyst Michael Ledeen.

♦ ♦ ♦

"Do they stay deprogrammed?" Poppa asks.

"Yeah, the last job—I've got some tapes here of the last gal that he deprogrammed. She thinks Galen is a god," Moore responds.

"Is he a young guy, this guy Galen?" Poppa wants to know.

"Hell, no, he's older than I am," said Moore, a man in his mid-40s.

"Is he really?"

"Big guy, about 6′3″."

"Is he really?"

"Nice guy. You know, you can see that he's got the psychologist in him," Moore says, admiringly.

"Right," Poppa responds.

"And we've just—we've always worked very well together. We think alike and it just was a natural formation of things to do."

"Right."

"And when I got fired, you know, Galen was still working part-time for Newbold. He said, 'A lot of people been waiting for you to come out.' What I discovered was, I have a sum of knowledge that nobody else has."

"Most of these people that he's gotten out, you've gotten out, most of them stayed normal or they go back into the—" Poppa asks. He wants to hear more about deprogramming, and less about what Moore thinks of himself.

"No, no they stay normal. They're my best friends. I've had them over—a week before, I had Chris Curtis over. You met him."

◆ ◆ ◆

Curtis, a former associate of LaRouche, had betrayed his friends in the LaRouche movement. Seeking to avoid prosecution, Curtis then became a key government witness, lying for the prosecution against LaRouche in several trials. As it turned out, Moore had taken care of Curtis, helping him, among other things, to secure admission to Virginia's George Mason University law school. Curtis had been paid by Newbold Smith to spy on Lewis Smith in New Hampshire in 1988.

"Is he deprogrammed?" Poppa asks.

"Yes!" Moore answers.

"Oh, he was," Poppa says, adding, "there's no chance of him swinging back, right?"

"No," Moore says. "Matter of fact, Chris is now getting his law degree. And, my friend, I will tell you this: Should I be elected Sheriff, I am creating a LaRouche investigative organization, and Chris Curtis is going to be part of that."

Moore continues to spin his fantasy about what he will do once he's elected Loudoun County Sheriff; that his LaRouche investigative unit will operate like the pacification programs he ran back in Vietnam. "We got some Viet Cong out, turned them around and used them as scouts. A couple of LaRouchies I know real well—ex-LaRouchies deprogrammed. I'm going to send back in, and those guys won't sleep at night trying to get back. One thing about LaRouche people, all of them do, they are incredible workers. They will not sleep. I used to joke that they were like the old Japanese soldiers. They would fight all day on a bag of rice. Markham said it best. He said, 'In order to fight and arrest fanatics, you are going to have to become a fanatic yourself.' " Moore waxes nostalgic about the LaRouche prosecutions, and former LaRouche prosecutor John Markham.

The conversation drones on. The two men start exchanging police stories again. Poppa listens as Moore tells of beating people up when he was a park police officer in Fairfax County, Virginia. As they near Philadelphia, Moore underscores what worries him most about this line of work: getting caught.

◆ ◆ ◆

"When anything goes down, three people have to be standing next to Mother Theresa: myself, Galen Kelly and Newbold Smith," Moore says.

"Right."

"Well, in other words, the LaRouchies would absolutely in a minute, you know, if the FBI said, 'Well, who would wanna kidnap him?' It would be Newbold Smith and Don Moore and Galen Kelly."

"Do the LaRouchies know you up here?"

"No, they don't. But they would simply toss that name in the pot, because they believe that I'm like this master planner. You know, I'm this nefarious agent. They still have yet to find out I went to Israel. If they find that out, they'll write a whole new chapter in their book."

"Right," Poppa says.

"Well, like I say, I'm gonna be standing with Mother Theresa when this thing goes down. I'm going to be like, you know, all three of us are going to be testifying on the Hill, Capitol Hill." Moore laughs out loud, happy and secure that he'll have "plausible deniability."

At 1:30 in the morning, they finally arrive at Newbold's mansion in Radnor, Pennsylvania. Poppa's tired, but he and his tape recorder have learned a lot.

6 | Garbologist First, Investigator Second

As dawn breaks on the morning of July 8, Don Moore is fast asleep. He's tired from talking his head off the whole ride up. By this time, Doug Poppa needs some fresh air and some fresh tapes, so he wakes up early and takes the opportunity to go for a jog. Once out of the house, he meets an FBI agent who's providing him cover. He gives the agent his used tapes, gets some fresh ones, and jogs back to the house. He's back in bed before Moore even stirs.

After eating breakfast, Poppa and Moore leave Newbold Smith's mansion to go conduct the surveillance of Lewis and Andrea Smith. The purpose is to determine the daily routine of the couple, information necessary in preparation for the planned kidnapping. The Eastern States Distributors (ESDI) office, where Lewis and Andrea volunteer their time as political organizers, is located on the second floor of a row of storefronts on a quiet street in the working-class suburb of Upper Darby. The two men take positions up the street. Moore is careful to keep his distance, for fear someone might recognize him.

Poppa ventures closer in order to get the license plate numbers of the cars parked in front of the building.

While Moore and Poppa watch the movements of Lewis, Andrea and their colleagues, an FBI surveillance team watches Moore and Poppa.

The two men make careful observations of Lewis's routine, taking photographs of the building. They watch as Lewis goes into the Irish Pub restaurant after work. They follow him to the Wanamaker apartment house in downtown Philadelphia, where Lewis and Andrea are living while they prepare to move into their new home.

At night, Moore and Poppa go to the house in Chestnut Hill. The house is still empty. Moore takes this as confirmation of his concocted story that the house is really going to be an office for ESDI. While Poppa waits in the car, Moore goes onto the property and looks in the windows. Suddenly, a neighbor, sensing an intruder on the property of the vacant house, turns on an outside light and yells. Startled but undaunted, Moore scurries back to the car.

Finished with their day of snooping, they go back to Newbold's mansion for the night.

The next morning, Moore sends Poppa out to conduct the surveillance alone so he can stay behind at Newbold's. Instead, Poppa goes straight to the FBI regional office in Newtown Square, near Upper Darby, where he meets Special Agent Gregory J. Alt.

While Poppa's on his way to the FBI office, Newbold Smith calls Moore from his house in Maine to get a report on how the kidnap preparations are going.

At 1:15 p.m. Poppa, still at the FBI office, calls Moore at the Smith mansion. Ramona, the maid, answers the phone. There's a long pause. All Poppa hears is the sound of Newbold's dog. He waits. Finally, Moore picks up the phone. He sounds as if he's just awakened.

"Yeah, the Cadillac's here," Poppa says, referring to Lewis's car. He speaks as if he's calling from outside ESDI's office in Upper Darby. "Yeah, just some of the same people coming and going like yesterday."

Sounding dazed, Moore tells Poppa to come back to the house for lunch.

Using the evidence Poppa has gathered so far, the FBI prepares to get an order for a wiretap on Newbold's home phone in Radnor.

In the evening, Moore and Poppa watch the Irish bar again and return to Newbold's house.

At 10:45 p.m., based on an affidavit from the FBI stating that Newbold Smith, Don Moore and Galen Kelly are conspiring to kidnap Lewis and Andrea Smith, U.S. District Judge Edmund Ludwig signs an order authorizing a wiretap on the elder Smith's phone.

Simultaneously, FBI agents in Alexandria, Virginia obtain an order from U.S. District Judge Claude Hilton for a wiretap on Moore's home phone in Lovettsville, Virginia.

The next morning, as Moore and Poppa are eating breakfast, the FBI is installing the wiretap. Within 20 minutes of the activation of the tap, the phone rings and Poppa answers, because Moore is in the shower. It's Newbold Smith calling. He wants to talk to Moore.

◆ ◆ ◆

"I've got good news for you." Newbold Smith is excited. "Once in a while your brain works, or, mine does. And I finally thought to myself, you know something, said I to myself, that female lawyer that I spoke to you about?"

"Oh?" Moore's curiosity is piqued.

"And if she wrote me a letter would I have thrown that out? Hell, no. I would have filed it in the Lewis file. So, ten minutes ago, I called my office, got my secretary to go into the file. She pulled out the letter and told me, told me the name of the person who sent the letter to me, the name of the law firm. I called up the law firm. I asked for the lawyer. She's out. She's calling me back within an hour."

"Excellent."

"Now the suit is—just so you don't have to go over this," Newbold continues.

"All right. Let me, let me get a pen and paper. Stand by," Moore says.

"Okay, the person who got ripped off was named Herbert Royer, and the person doing the suing is either daughter or niece, I think maybe daughter. Her name is Ann Coleman of Stamford, Connecticut. So my memory served me on the Connecticut thing. The name of the law firm is Kohn, Klein, Nast and Graf. The name of the lady lawyer, who's handling the case entirely herself, according to her secretary, is Deborah Sottosanti," Newbold finishes.

Ann Coleman and her sister Margaret Kostopolous are active in CAN. Margaret has worked with Galen Kelly personally, and Kelly has been in contact with Sottosanti while she has been preparing the lawsuit. Harold Kohn, the chief partner in the law firm, is known as the godfather of the class action suit. He is a multi-million-dollar lawyer infamous for his ruthless tactics and high fees. A contributor and supporter of the ADL, Kohn has been the long-time lawyer for Walter Annenberg, the Philadelphia media magnate whose family wire service business was built with the help of Meyer Lansky's mob.

Newbold thinks this could be a breakthrough, asking if his son, Lewis Smith, ought to be included as a defendant in the woman's suit. "Now, I want you to understand something. If one of the things that happens is that they get a judgment against Lewis, I've thought this through. That's perfectly okay," Newbold says.

While Poppa goes out to do more surveillance, Moore contacts Sottosanti right away, introducing himself by saying, "Let me explain my background. I was the deputy sheriff who started not only the Virginia but the federal cases in Loudoun County. Leesburg was in my jurisdiction, and you may or may not have run into my name."

"Oh, I have many times," Sottosanti assures Moore.

"Okay, all right. So then I don't need to go into any great detail."

"No, you don't have to. That's fine. I've spoken with the people out in Waynesboro—Mrs. Overington."

"Ah, so," Moore says.

◆ ◆ ◆

Helen Overington used to be an active political and financial supporter of the LaRouche movement. When LaRouche associate Rochelle Ascher was unjustly convicted of securities law violations in 1989 and given a barbaric 86-year sentence by Virginia Judge Carleton Penn (which he later reduced to ten years), Mrs. Overington wrote a letter to the judge vigorously denouncing the sentence. Yet one year later, after intensive sessions with CAN deprogrammers, Mrs. Overington withdrew her support.

Pressure was brought on Mrs. Overington because her daughters, Mary Rotz and Peggy Weller, and her son, John Overington, opposed her political views, and wanted her money. Mrs. Overington's children first called the

Virginia Attorney General's office, which referred the matter to C.D. Bryant, the chief LaRouche investigator for the Virginia State Police, and a former federal Internal Revenue Service supervisor.

Bryant later testified in court that he referred the family to Mira Lansky Boland, the LaRouche case officer for the Anti-Defamation League, because the family believed Mrs. Overington had been "brainwashed." Boland in turn put the family in touch with CAN. Soon, Mrs. Overington's children moved her from her apartment in Baltimore, where she had been living on her own, into a house next to her daughter in Pennsylvania; there, Mrs. Overington found herself under virtual house arrest. She was worked on by Boland, CAN's then-president, Rev. Michael Rokos, and Bryant, who all told her lies, slanders, and half-truths about LaRouche and his associates. Mrs. Overington resisted the pressure for some days, refusing to believe the lies. She later told the news media that her family had to work on her pretty hard before she would believe she had been "brainwashed" when she supported LaRouche.

In a January 1991 article in *Woman's Day* magazine, Helen Overington described her political disagreements with her family: "When I tried to talk politics with my children, they'd say, 'Oh, Mom, you really don't believe that stuff, do you?' or 'Oh, Mom, you've been reading all that conservative literature again.' Especially Peggy, the most liberal. She finally told me, 'Look, Mom, we can't discuss these things. We just don't agree.'"

In an interview with an investigator, Peggy Overington Weller said her mother was deprogrammed with the help of CAN.

The Overington children also teamed up with Newbold Smith to organize and fund the "LaRouche Victims Support Group" which specifically targets supporters of LaRouche. The group has a special phone number in CAN's office so that callers can be referred to Kelly and other "experts" on LaRouche.

Once Mrs. Overington had been "deprogrammed," her family tried to use her to extort money from Rochelle Ascher, threatening to testify against Ascher in a criminal proceeding if Ascher didn't pay Overington some money. The family hired the Harrisburg, Pennsylvania law firm of McNees Wallace, which had worked with the ADL and CAN in a previous case. When Ascher's attorney exposed the extortion attempt, McNees Wallace dropped out of the case.

The CAN-directed Overingtons also sought revenge by launching a national media campaign through journalists sympathetic to CAN and the ADL, such as Patricia Lynch of NBC News. John Overington, a West Virginia state legislator, sent CAN's hate literature, under his official letterhead, to every state legislature in the country, seeking to harass LaRouche supporters by instigating bogus legal proceedings. Overington also proposed legislation which would effectively outlaw political fund-raising.

One such bill actually passed the Maryland General Assembly in 1992. The law puts unconstitutional restrictions on political and charitable fundraising. It passed after the legislature held hearings at which Galen Kelly and CAN provided most of the testimony.

◆ ◆ ◆

Moore offers to help Sottosanti. "Now, okay. Well, at that point, I had come up here to do a surveillance on the

Upper Darby office up here with a friend of mine who's also involved in the same dispute with a sheriff down there. So we are both folks who have had some talent in this, but by the same token, we were free to play our own game. I had asked Newbold to try and locate you folks through several ways of going about it, with the idea that there were probably some commonalities of interest and moreover, there were certain bits of information that I may already have, that you don't need to necessarily invent the wheel," Moore states.

"Now, there's a third thing that's involved here. CAN, the Cult Awareness Network, is also in the process of starting a suit against LaRouchies for defamation of character and other things," Moore says.

"Yeah, they've been pretty tough on CAN," Sottosanti interjects.

"And what has happened is, I just got done helping Cynthia Kisser locate corporate documents. She wanted to find the entities necessary to sue, to basically go up the chain of command, and I was able to locate the documents she wanted, and I Fedexed those up to her at the beginning of the week. My point is, that at some point I think there's probably a commonality of interest both from an information standpoint, and perhaps productivity at the other end, which I would like at some point to see if you and maybe Newbold's lawyer, and Cynthia Kisser, etc., could sit down and discuss at some point, wherein we don't have to reinvent the wheel. I think there's probably things I can help you with, and since I live just outside of Leesburg, there are things that can be accomplished at that end," Moore offers.

"Okay," Sottosanti says.

Moore continues, "Are you aware that a federal jury

in Virginia, when they first indicted Lyndon LaRouche, the very first indictment had a RICO indictment, and the prosecutors decided against it because of the politics involved?"

Sottosanti responds, "Yeah, well, I've spoken with, oh, I'm not remembering anybody's names, because I've put them aside for a little bit—"

"Kent Robinson?" Moore asks, referring to the Alexandria federal prosecutor of LaRouche.

"Oh, shoot, the Anti-Defamation League," Sottosanti continues.

"Oh, Mira Boland," Moore says.

"Yes, yes. She gave me some of the background," Sottosanti says.

Moore offers her the inside information he has obtained by rummaging through the trash dumpsters outside the offices of LaRouche's associates in Leesburg.

"Boy, trash can be interesting, huh?" Sottosanti asks.

"Yeah. Garbologist first, investigator second," Moore boasts.

Moore then brags about his work on the LaRouche cases. He brags about the lengthy sentences given in Virginia to LaRouche associates, for convictions on securities law violations. "[Michael] Billington got 77 years and took the full 77 in the head. He'll be a wrinkled prune when he gets out, if he does," Moore gloats.

◆ ◆ ◆

Michael Billington is an associate of LaRouche, who was convicted in 1988 with LaRouche in the federal railroad trial in Alexandria. Despite the federal conviction, the state of Virginia also prosecuted Billington on virtually the same charges in 1989—a violation of the constitutional ban on double jeopardy.

Billington's Virginia trial was a sham. His own lawyer, Brian Gettings, turned against him the day before his trial was to begin. Gettings tried to have Billington declared mentally incompetent, because Billington insisted on his right to a jury trial. Then, the presiding judge, Roanoke Circuit Court Judge Clifford R. Weckstein (a close friend of the ADL), refused to let Billington fire Gettings and hire a new lawyer.

In the trial that followed, Gettings failed to adequately defend Billington. He was convicted, and the jury sentenced him to a barbaric 77-year sentence on securities law violations. Judge Weckstein compounded the outrage by refusing to reduce the sentence.

◆ ◆ ◆

Concluding his conversation with Debbie Sottosanti, Moore also offers her access to several "defectors" from the LaRouche movement, especially Chris Curtis. "If there is some way that interests can be commingled here, it would be of benefit on both sides, or actually all three including CAN," Moore concludes, and Sottosanti agrees.

When in the early afternoon Poppa comes back to Newbold Smith's house, Moore fills him in on his discussions with Newbold and Sottosanti. He's also been looking for Galen Kelly, because Newbold wants Kelly involved in anything they do. "A couple of things happened," Moore says, "I told you about Galen, Galen Kelly; big guy—Galen somehow or another put his dick in the wringer."

"Uh huh."

"He's got a lawyer, he's called 'Biker Bob.' Greatest

guy you ever want to meet. He's a lawyer, but he's also a biker," Moore explains.

"Right."

"And he operates out of Perth Amboy, New Jersey."

"Right."

"And Biker Bob cleans up Galen's messes."

Robert "Biker Bob" Point is a 300-pound former South Amboy, New Jersey policeman who got his law degree after being injured in a drug bust. Point practices law out of a storefront in South Amboy, where he's the town's zoning lawyer. But he also does work for CAN, providing "legal" cover for Kelly.

Moore says he called Point from Newbold's phone to get a message to Kelly that he and Newbold want to consult with him. If Kelly remains out of touch, Moore plans to continue on his own with the preparations.

At 3:45 in the afternoon, the two men start the drive back to Leesburg. On the way, Poppa asks, "So what's the story with Galen now? He's out of the picture, or is he coming in?"

Moore responds, "Well he's out of the picture for right now and maybe for the foreseeable future. He's definitely gonna have to be brought in for the deprogramming or whatever we finally decide to do. We can't do the whole thing without him. He's got to deprogram him," Moore says, referring to kidnap victim Lewis Smith, "but when we snatch him, you know, we can do the whole tactical thing without him."

EIRNS/Philip Ulanowsky

The paymaster of the conspiracy, E. Newbold Smith, center, flanked by his wife, Peggy (right), and attorney John Markham (left) following Smith's acquittal for conspiring to kidnap his son, Lewis. Markham was a former assistant U.S. Attorney who prosecuted Lyndon LaRouche in the same Alexandria federal courthouse in 1988.

◀ Former Loudoun County, Va. Sheriff's Deputy Donald Moore, with his wife, Janine, outside the Alexandria federal courthouse.

EIRNS/Stuart Lewis

EIRNS/Philip Ulanowsky

EIRNS/Stuart Lewis

▲ Ex-cop Tony Russo

◄ CAN's professional kidnapper/
deprogrammer Galen Kelly

▼ Galen Kelly's attorney, Robert
"Biker Bob" Point

EIRNS/Stuart Lewis

▶ Lewis du Pont Smith and Andrea Diano were married in December 1986 in a Catholic Church ceremony in Rome, Italy. Lyndon LaRouche (right) was best man.

▼ Lewis du Pont Smith, with his wife, Andrea, at his side, announces for Congress in New Hampshire in 1988.

EIRNS

EIRNS/Don Mallory

◀ Doug Poppa, the former Loudoun County, Va. Sheriff's Deputy who captured the Kidnappers, Inc. conspirators on FBI surveillance tapes. Prosecutor Larry Leiser called Poppa "a hero."

▼ Government prosecutors who tried the Kidnappers, Inc. case, from right to left: Assistant U.S. Attorney John Martin, Assistant U.S. Attorney Larry Leiser, and FBI agent Scott Salter.

EIRNS/Philip Ulanowsky

EIRNS/Philip Ulanowsky

Then-Sheriff's Deputy Don Moore (left) shepherds ex-LaRouche associate Criton Zoakos to Lyndon LaRouche's sentencing, January 1989.

Ex-LaRouche associate Chris Curtis (third from left), on his way to testify against LaRouche associate Rochelle Ascher in Loudoun County, Va., in March 1989. The blur at right is Don Moore, trying to keep photographers away from his "deprogrammed" protegé.

EIRNS/Philip Ulanowsky

▲ Former LaRouche associates Freyda and Bobby Greenberg, shown here at the federal courthouse in Boston in 1988, where Greenberg was a defendant in the Boston federal "LaRouche case."

► Former LaRouche associate Paul Greenberg, Bobby Greenberg's brother, who was convicted with LaRouche and five others in Alexandria federal court in 1988—thanks in large part to Don Moore.

EIRNS/Stuart Lewis

EIRNS/Stuart Lewis

Bryan Chitwood right, the Loudoun Times-Mirror reporter and notorious drunk, who authored Don Moore-inspired slanders of the LaRouche movement in the small Virginia community of Loudoun County. To his left is another of Don Moore's snitches, Loudoun Times-Mirror photographer Doug Graham. Graham's wife, Dawn, worked in a local camera store, and illegally gave Moore copies of photos taken by LaRouche associates.

EIRNS/Stuart Lewis

Local eccentric and then-member of the County Board of Supervisors Frank Raflo, in 1986 hid behind his copy of ADL hate literature slandering the LaRouche movement.

EIRNS/Stuart Lewis

▲ Frank Raflo throws a bag of rocks on the floor during the 1985 public hearing on a summer camp LaRouche associates hoped to operate in Loudoun County, Va. The population had been whipped up by Raflo, Don Moore, and others to believe rumors that the camp, Sweetwater Farm, was a terrorist training center.

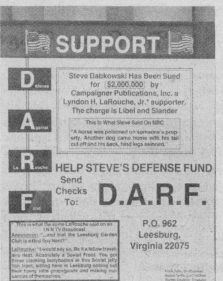

SUPPORT

D **A** **R** **F**

Steve Dabkowski Has Been Sued for $2,000,000 by Campaigner Publications, Inc. a Lyndon H. LaRouche, Jr.* supporter. The charge is Libel and Slander

This is What Steve Said On NBC

"A horse was poisoned on someone's property. Another dog came home with his tail cut off and his back, hind legs skinned."

HELP STEVE'S DEFENSE FUND

Send Checks To: **D.A.R.F.**

P.O. 962 Leesburg, Virginia 22075

This is what the same LaRouche said on an I N N TV Broadcast Announcer: "...and that the Leesburg Garden Club is a Red Spy Nest?" LaRouche: "I would say so. Be it a fellow travelers Nest. Absolutely a Soviet Front. You got these clocking bunnybodies in this Soviet jellyfish front, sitting here in Leesburg oozing out their funny little propaganda and making nuisances of themselves."

◄ A leaflet put out by a Loudoun County group formed by Don Moore's snitches, called DARF. DARF was set up to retail slanders against LaRouche and his associates, such as that the "LaRouchies" mutilated animals.

EIRNS/Stuart Lewis

7 | We Can't Do a God Damn Thing Until We Get Galen

On July 11, Doug Poppa calls Don Moore to find out what's next, after the surveillance trip to Philadelphia. Moore wants to keep Poppa's interest, but there's one major hitch that's keeping their plans on hold: Galen Kelly's still hiding out.

"You know, basically, I'm still waiting for my friend in the woods, and when he staggers on out, we need to do some consulting. Not that he's the end-all and be-all, it's just we've always consulted before, and you know, it's worked out, so we're gonna do it again," Moore laments.

While waiting for Kelly, Moore wants to keep up the surveillance. He assigns Poppa the job of finding a good place from which to take pictures of the quarry, Lewis Smith. " 'Cause I got the lens that will do it, man. I got some stuff that you haven't seen yet that will show you a pubic hair on an ant at 500 yards in a rainstorm. So I got bigger stuff than they ever had down there," Moore brags.

They wait and they wait. At 9:00 a.m. on July 15, Moore gets a call from Newbold Smith.

Newbold's been trying to reach Kelly, but to no avail.

He's only spoken with Kelly's wife, Liz. Newbold is impatient. He wants the kidnapping, but he knows it can't succeed without Kelly's direction.

"I really think that Galen is pivotal right here," Newbold says. "I think we can't do a God damn thing until we get Galen."

"That question—I think I'm safe—I'm sure I'm safe here," Newbold says, wondering out loud if his phone is tapped.

"Uh huh, yeah. I'm safe here. I'm safe here," Moore assures him, not suspecting the FBI's tape recorders are picking up the whole conversation.

"Okay," Newbold begins, now that he thinks no one else is listening. "Uh, let's say he's lifted."

"Yeah."

"Uh, then the big concern is, she's screaming," Newbold says, referring to Lewis's wife, Andrea.

"Uh huh."

"First—well, point number one, it's preferable to lift him without her, is it not?" Newbold asks.

"That is a Galen question." Moore defers to the expert.

"I know."

"That is uh, that's one—I have my own thought process on that—but I think that's a Galen question."

"Well, but I'm assuming you and Galen have talked about it."

"Yeah."

"Let me change the question. Let me rephrase it. Presuming it is your collective decision, that lifting him is preferable to lifting them both, then you've got an adversary back here," Newbold persists.

"Uh huh."

"Uh, I, I'm sure you must have considered, um, evasive type things—maneuvers to make it look like somebody from within is doing this, or—something like that. Because I think that, um, if she somehow could be diverted and suspect somebody other than Lewis' family behind this thing—I'm not thinking for my own skin point of view. I'm just thinking from the God damn thing working point of view." Newbold is getting impatient. "So all I'm saying is, you guys have thought through all those processes, have you not?" he asks.

"Yes, and, and, some of those are questions within questions that, uh, for example, uh, uh, at some point—" Moore says, trying to reassure Newbold he's on top of the situation, while revealing that he's not.

But Kelly is unavailable, so they can't decide whether to kidnap Lewis alone or take Andrea, too. Newbold is frustrated. "Hell, I may end up saying screw it, let the, let the lad go his own way for the rest of his life. It, it's, it's a chicken way of thinking, but—" he says disappointedly, because he doesn't want to give up.

"I think it's gonna require a meeting of—lengthy meeting, uh, you, me and Galen," Newbold resolves.

Moore says he'll continue to try and arrange a meeting with Kelly through Bob Point. Perhaps a clandestine meeting can be arranged.

"And if it comes down to it, if Galen has a problem, uh, what I may pass on to Bob is, hey, uh, Galen could just show up at the house, you know. I mean, he doesn't have to utilize electronic communications, if he's got a problem. You know, uh, you know, he just within a period of x, y and z, he shows up at the house."

"He can hold up here for a while, if he wants to," Newbold offers.

◆ ◆ ◆

Moore tries repeatedly to reach Kelly. He calls Kelly's wife, and he leaves messages with "Biker Bob," but Kelly still isn't ready to "stagger out of the woods."

Moore knows that Kelly will eventually surface, but it's been two weeks since he and Poppa were in Philadelphia. He needs some new information. He doesn't know whether Lewis and Andrea have moved into their new house, and he needs to find out if there has been any change in their daily routine. Whenever Kelly finally emerges, Moore wants to be ready.

Meanwhile, Poppa is keeping busy with the Carter retrial back in Leesburg, at which he is a key defense witness. Then, in late July, after Carter's trial has ended with his acquittal, Moore asks Poppa to go back to Philadelphia and do the surveillance himself.

"I'll give ya my big lens and one of the cameras and a tripod." Moore wants Poppa to take surveillance photographs.

"Don't give me that fucking thing that looks like a bazooka," Poppa protests, "the thing you took out that day."

"Yeah, right, but you put that thing up in that telephone room and you're gonna be counting their pubic hairs when they walk around the corner," Moore brags.

Moore says Poppa can stay at Newbold's mansion, the maid will be there.

"And nobody else?" Poppa asks.

"Well, may or may not be. I mean, they could be up there in Maine or not, but you'll get along both ways," Moore says. He tells Poppa what to expect, if and when he meets Newbold. "You know he's an old crusty bastard, he sounds like Mr. Magoo." Moore describes the elder Smith aptly.

"Really?"

"Yeah, he, he's tall, about six, six, six foot."

"Okay."

"But, you know, pushing seventy, has a problem walking, has maybe one or two drinks in the evening too much."

"Right."

"But you'll do well, I mean, you've got to learn to start talking to these people with money, man. You've been dealing with the dirt so long you forgot how to talk to humans," Moore admonishes.

"I can talk to human people," Poppa corrects.

"Oh, yeah? You could fool me."

Moore cautions Poppa further how to act if Smith is there. "Listen, you don't need to discuss snatching anybody, okay?" Moore warns.

"Right."

"Uh, with Newbold. 'Cause that's, that's basically a closely held plan, you understand. Basically, what you understand from this whole thing is, you're doing this thing for me because you're good on the streets."

"Right."

"And that at some point we're gonna introduce a psychiatrist or somebody named Galen into this thing, in order to meet with his son. And that's all you care for right now," Moore says.

Poppa wants to make sure he understands what Moore has just said. "Okay, so let me get this. Okay, so if he starts talking, then I give him the impression that I don't know anything about snatching his son."

"You got it."

"And that the only thing I know about Galen is he's a psychiatrist," Poppa adds.

"Either a psychiatrist or deprogrammer, something, you don't know," Moore clarifies. "But it's something to do with that and that there's gonna be a psychological meeting of the minds at some point where Galen—"

"But we actually know," Poppa interrupts, "I'm supposed to give the impression to him that I know what he knows."

"You got it exactly," Moore assures him.

"So I got to play like, semi-stupid," Poppa says, tongue in cheek.

"Not semi-stupid, you can do that naturally, I'm just saying, well, not knowledgeable," Moore says, not missing the opportunity to insult Poppa.

Poppa wants to make sure he's got this on the FBI's tape. "I'm supposed to give him the impression that I only know so much."

"Right."

"So I wanna make sure I don't run my fucking mouth."

"You got it exactly."

"So the only thing I know is that I'm down there—"

"Is to put these bastards away," Moore finishes the sentence for him.

"To put the LaRouche people away. Listen, to put the LaRouche people away," Poppa repeats.

"Yeah," Moore approves.

"And that I know nothing about the snatching of the son," Poppa says again.

"You got it exactly," Moore assures him. "And that's the only subject you've got to stay off of."

"The snatching of the son," answers Poppa. He

presses once more for clarification. "Well, let me ask a stupid question, since I'm on the right track here. But he knows actually what's going on?" he asks, referring to Newbold.

"Right," Moore says.

"But I gotta give him the impression that—"

"You don't know," instructs Moore.

"I don't know what's going on."

"That's right," Moore again approves.

8 I'm Trying to Start A War Against LaRouche Again

Galen Kelly's absence may have put on hold the implementation of the kidnap plans, but Don Moore isn't about to let that interfere with his obsession to destroy the LaRouche movement. Moore is looking for every opportunity to stir up trouble for his enemy.

Moore's first chance comes when he gets back from vacation. On August 2, he gets an unexpected call from Rick Munson, an investigator for Minnesota Attorney General Hubert "Skip" Humphrey III. Humphrey, the son of the late Vice President Hubert Humphrey, has a longstanding, deep personal hatred for LaRouche. And since at least 1986, he has repeatedly used his office to launch political attacks on LaRouche and his associates.

Unlike Moore, Humphrey's hatred for LaRouche is hereditary. His father's political career was built with the help of Meyer Lansky's Midwest organized crime syndicate headed by Isadore Blumenfeld, also known as "Kid Cann," and his two brothers, Harry and Yiddy Bloom. During Prohibition, Minnesota was a major transshipment point for illegal whiskey coming from Canada, and was a center for gambling and bookmaking operations.

Gangsters from all over the United States found a safe haven in the Minneapolis-St. Paul area during the 1920s and '30s. These were the same organized crime families that became the leaders of the ADL. When the elder Humphrey ran his first race for mayor of Minneapolis, his campaign manager was the mother of Burton Joseph, a man who later became national chairman of the Anti-Defamation League.

"Skip" Humphrey's contributors' list reads like a Who's Who of organized crime figures and ADL moneybags. In 1986, after two LaRouche supporters won primary elections in Illinois, AG Humphrey used his muscle in the state's Democratic Farmer Labor Party to blackball LaRouche supporters from the party.

Being a creature of such organized crime circles, "Skip" Humphrey had no problem flouting the law, and dealing with those of criminal mindset, such as Don Moore. In early 1991, Rick Munson and Moore teamed up to illegally obtain search and seizure warrants for bank accounts and financial records of the Constitutional Defense Fund, an organization providing legal defense support for LaRouche and his associates. Also targetted were some publishing companies which produced literature for the LaRouche political movement. When three separate judges in Minnesota, Pennsylvania and Virginia found out that Munson and Moore had lied to obtain the warrants, the warrants were thrown out.

♦ ♦ ♦

"Well, boy. A voice out of the past," Moore says, when Rick Munson identifies himself on the phone.

"Listen, we're still working this LaRouche deal," Munson says.

"That is amazing," Moore says excitedly.

"I don't know if you knew that."

"No, I thought it had been shut down," Moore says.

"No, we had been sued by them as well. I myself personally, and the prosecutor and also the attorney general. And we were sued in Pennsylvania over these warrants that we did, that freeze their bank accounts and get bank records." Munson explains.

"I figured this thing had been shut down," Moore says again.

"Oh, hell no. In fact, we're on the verge of charging at least one of their members, and maybe two here in the next two or three weeks, probably." Munson says the original case he and Moore had worked on had fallen through, but that they were now developing another case.

"First of all, I need to bring you up on some history here. In 25 words or less I'm no longer working for the Sheriff's office," Moore says.

"Oh, okay," Munson sounds disappointed.

"All right. That doesn't mean a thing because I'm still conducting LaRouche investigations," Moore boasts, adding, "I am basically working for an outfit that is out of Chicago called CAN, Cult Awareness Network. I still do the same things, but I no longer have law enforcement powers down here."

Moore gives Munson a very abbreviated report on the shakeout in the Loudoun County Sheriff's office. "Right now we are awaiting, as a matter of fact, word that the Sheriff may in fact resign. If that occurs I will be running on the Republican ticket, since the Sheriff was a Democrat."

"Great."

"And I will have, to tell you, more than a reasonable chance of winning. In which case should that occur, it's open season on Mr. LaRouche," Moore vows.

As the two men talk, they renew their alliance against LaRouche. Moore offers to share information he obtained while he was a Deputy Sheriff. He tells Munson that "virtually all the documentation is still with me now. I have some 16 file cabinets full of information. The reason why I was—towards the end, I realized that—were frankly some serious problems in what we call our CID section. So basically, since it was my case and since it had never been given a case number, I took the documents home. And guess what? The local prosecutor ruled I had every right to do so. It was my work product. We have a different set of rules here in Virginia."

"Yeah, we couldn't do that here," Munson says.

"Yeah. Well, we have a work product rule. We're very primitive down here. You get to take your ball and go home. You may get sent home by the coach, but you get to take the ball."

"What a mess," Munson commiserates.

"You probably think you're talking to a legal cave man, and you're right. We've got big clubs out here." Moore brags about the infamous barbarism of a Virginia judicial system which has successfully refused, unlike most other states, to follow the U.S. Code. Virginia is one of the few states to allow jury sentencing. And, until 1985, there was no appeals court. There is no automatic right to appeal a conviction; that right is granted by the appeals court.

Virginia also allows persons to be tried in state court for the same crime for which they have already been tried in federal court—double jeopardy, prohibited by the U.S. Constitution. As well, Virginia has become the number one death penalty state, executing more prisoners per capita than any other state in the United States, including Texas.

"As far as I'm concerned, the enemy of my enemy is my friend," Moore says. "You know, that's what the Arabs say, and if you guys are all marching upstream to take them out up there in Chicago, hell, man, when the thing's over, I can give you the name of a couple of TV reporters who owe me big time for the story when LaRouche took out the Illinois primary. There are some people there that would give me an arm just to have a story to whack these people with. So if you're looking for friendly faces, I've got plenty of them."

"Well, that's fabulous and we'd sure like to get these guys," Munson says, sharing Moore's enthusiasm.

As soon as Munson hangs up, Moore is on the phone to CAN's headquarters in Chicago. Hearing that Cynthia Kisser is on another call, he leaves a message: "Tell her I have information about criminal prosecutions to occur at Midwestern Circulation Corporation and I need to talk to her in probably the next 15 minutes or so."

He says eagerly, "We need to get a commonality of interests going here, all righty?"

Moore wants Kisser to send him copies of her suit against the LaRouche movement right away, so Doug Poppa can serve the papers on the people Kisser is suing.

◆ ◆ ◆

While waiting for Kisser to call back, Moore calls Bob O'Harrow, an eager-beaver young Loudoun County bureau reporter for the *Washington Post*. Moore is operating on instinct. The *Post* played a major role in the prosection of LaRouche, serving as an important vehicle for the prosecutors to circulate unproven allegations and outright lies before and during the trial. Government prosecutors found this essential, because it created such a polluted jury pool that it was impossible to find jurors who had not been influenced by the *Post*'s anti-LaRouche coverage.

Without such a polluted jury pool, it would have been difficult, if not impossible, to obtain the convictions of LaRouche and his associates. O'Harrow was now Moore's main contact at the *Post*.

Moore tells O'Harrow about his conversation with Munson. He promises to make copies of the complaints available for the press.

"It represents a commonality of interest for me because of my work for CAN. CAN is getting ready to sue the LaRouche organization for libel." Moore tells O'Harrow he plans to use CAN's civil case as a way to circumvent the Fifth Amendment rights against self-incrimination of the people Minnesota plans to charge.

"Now, what I am trying to do—this is off-record— what I am trying to do is to set it up so that as the lawsuit progresses on the civil side, they get to do what is known as depositions. They get to invite people in and sit down and ask them how the corporation works. That will be very beneficial to an organization that is trying to find what is known as business practice. If you're doing a criminal case where they wouldn't be necessarily subject to, you know, they might at that point want to claim it incriminates—Fifth Amendment. You can't do that in a civil case because it's not criminal." Moore instructs O'Harrow in the fine points of civil and criminal law.

"Right."

"You see what I'm saying?" Moore says. "So what goes through the front door, can often be obtained through the back door," Moore says proudly.

O'Harrow is grateful. Always on the lookout for a juicy story, he's more than willing to publish whatever Moore gives him. Moore sums it up.

"In the meantime, I need to talk to the CAN folks. And also there's another case that's operating, a RICO civil suit that is operating out of Philadelphia against the Eastern States Distributor, which is a LaRouche organization over there. So under the circumstances, what I'm saying is that what you're seeing is a sort of a colliding of planets for a second round at LaRouche."

"Well, that would be interesting. That would be interesting if we can get a local angle on that stuff," O'Harrow enthuses.

"So, ostensibly, I'm doing private work. What I'm trying to do is get a coalition of Minnesota working on Mideastern Distributors out of Chicago, along with CAN, who's going to be doing a libel suit and then doing a civil case of trustees of Lewis du Pont Smith and the Philadelphia AG's office working on Eastern States Distributors," Moore continues.

"What's the family's biggest concern?" O'Harrow asks, referring to Newbold Smith.

"Basically, that their son has had their money systematically stripped by the LaRouche organization. Moreover, and this hatred goes back a long way, one of the things the LaRouche organization did, and you may or may not remember this. Do you remember back one election ago when Pierre du Pont out of Delaware was trying to run for President? He was basically sabotaged by the LaRouche organization."

"Oh really?" O'Harrow says.

"Don't know that. And the Du Ponts were putting a lot of hope in Pierre for representing, frankly, the interests of the Du Pont family."

"Right."

"And they had submarined a lot of money into this thing. Well, he got whacked off real early," Moore claims, adding, "And a lot of it was done through Lewis du Pont Smith and the family, and coming up with a lot of family dirt that was spread around in the early primaries."

"Some of the LaRouchies are pretty smart. I mean, they are. They've got Ph.D.'s and stuff," O'Harrow interjects.

"Frankly if—let's put it this way. In cults, they are ideal candidates. You do not get your black, poor street dude in a cult. You get your Ph.D. Jewish guy from Swarthmore, who's looking to idealistically change the world, and who has had his mind opened to all new possibilities without being able to reject them out of hand. He has no critical negative reactions," says Moore, one of the ADL's favorite anti-Semites.

"Right," O'Harrow agrees.

"And so these guys, I mean, hell, they're nothing but potatoes on ice," Moore concludes.

"Pretty weird," O'Harrow responds. "Well, this is great stuff. I'm just curious this is like—"

"Every time I call you, I think I'm speaking from another planet, but believe me, there is a logic to all of this," Moore breaks in.

"Oh, no, listen, I'm all ears. You know, sometimes I just feel like I'm just sort of a sponge when we talk, I just feel like I need to soak up stuff," O'Harrow says, flattering Moore.

Moore's next call is to attorney Debbie Sottosanti in Philadelphia, who's working on a suit against associates of LaRouche, to which Moore and Newbold Smith want to add Lewis Smith, but she's not in. Moore can't wait, so he briefs her secretary on the latest developments in his anti-LaRouche operations, and arranges to call back later in the week.

♦ ♦ ♦

A few days pass before Moore and Poppa talk again.

"Some more LaRouche cases are popping up. A great case is popping up out of Minnesota," Moore says gleefully.

"Oh, really?"

"They're going to do some indictments and arrests in Chicago."

"Right," Poppa says.

"What I want to do is put together a case out of Philadelphia."

"Right."

"Against the Eastern States Distributors, at the same time that Cynthia Kisser is suing the Midwestern Distributors, which is basically a Chicago office. She's suing them for libel, and Minnesota is going for a couple of arrests."

"Right."

"You see what I'm trying to say? I'm trying to start a war against LaRouche again. All over the United States," Moore says triumphantly.

9 | Kidnapping—and Let's Call It What It Is

Although Don Moore has been back from vacation for over a week, everything is still on hold, waiting for Galen Kelly to surface. So Doug Poppa decides to do some investigating on his own. On August 10, he calls Moore, telling him he used to be a member of the Blue Knights Motorcycle Club and that the club is planning a barbecue in South Amboy, New Jersey. Poppa suggests he stop by to meet "Biker Bob" Point. Moore suggests Poppa might also try to meet Carol Hoffman, whom Moore refers to as the "poison bait" to be used to lure Lewis Smith into being kidnapped.

"She's not a hooker, is she?" Poppa asks.

"No, no, no, no. She's a daughter of a cop. She works an awful lot of P.I. type of cases, uh, and she's been working for Galen and, you know," Moore explains. "And if you're going up there, I'm gonna give Biker Bob a call and say, listen, there's one of my people—I just want him to face to face with you, no deep conversations, but, uh, you know, if you guys see each other in the hallway you need to know how to nod."

74

♦ ♦ ♦

The next day Poppa gets a call from Moore.

"What's happening?" Poppa asks.

"Well, uh, one thing not good, and another that's promising. Not good is that Newbold wants to hold off until the 18th. What he's doing is calling a confab of various people to meet. Um, he's got an idea, which frankly is good, and which I can't deny is good."

"What's that?" Poppa asks, curious.

"Uh, the girl's side of the family is Catholic." Moore says, referring to Lewis's wife, Andrea.

"Right."

"He's made contact with a Catholic priest who does deprogramming for the Catholic Church."

"Right."

"For cults."

"Right."

"Uh, he wants to get together and have me meet this Catholic guy. But the idea, if Galen is out of the picture, which may well be, 'cause he hasn't shown up," Moore says.

"Right."

"We need to go to plan two, and plan two may involve, uh, the Catholic Church approach through the Diano family."

"Right."

"And, uh, so, without doing any, uh—surveillance this week is out, but we may end up surveilling a—not a LaRouchie family but the family of the family, if you understand what I'm trying to say. The mother, the girl's side of the family," Moore continues. "With the idea of using the Catholic Church to make an approach to the

Catholic priest of Mrs. Diano."

"Right."

"So he's got a plan. It is a plan. You know we've had to sort of modify things due to Galen's disappearance," Moore says.

The Catholic priest Moore is talking about is not just some ordinary parish priest. He is Father James LeBar, of Hyde Park, New York, a member of the advisory board of both CAN and the American Family Foundation. Father LeBar is an activist in the deprogramming underground. Newbold Smith had previously consulted LeBar, seeking his help in trying to nullify Lewis and Andrea's marriage.

"Let me ask you a question," Poppa interjects.

"Sure."

"How is doing that to the girl going to get the other guy out of there?"

"If you get her out, you get him out," Moore asserts.

"Really?"

"The problem I've had all along is, especially right now, if kidnapping—and let's call it what it is—goes sour—"

"Right."

"It's gonna be very messy. And two, this is a big ass dude," Moore continues, referring to Lewis Smith, who had been a college football player.

"Right."

"So the chances of it being messy are extreme. You know, if, if—it would be easier to assassinate him than it would be to kidnap him," Moore blurts out.

"Right."

"And under the circumstances, what I am trying to

do is present a multiple of strategies that does not take us to that wall."

Poppa can't believe that Moore is so brazen, but the tape recorder has captured his every word.

◆ ◆ ◆

Two days later, when Moore and Poppa talk again, Moore says he and Newbold have still not talked to Kelly, but he plans to see Newbold on August 18. Moore urges Newbold to "try a Catholic Church thing. Rather than get stuck with, you know, waiting for Galen kind of thing."

"Wait—what if he just says—what if he agrees to go along, whatever—or they get her, you know—then how is that going to get him?" Poppa still doesn't understand if this new plan supersedes or supplements the kidnap plan that had already been discussed.

"Well, if we could get her cooperating in this process, even if it came down to a snatch," Moore explains, "if she doesn't go screaming to the feds, the others don't have any standing. You see what I'm trying to say? If she'd get to the point where she said, 'Hey, I agree with this thing. We need to get out and we can spend our own money.' "

"You mean, have her go along with the—" Poppa interrupts.

"Yeah. In other words, uh, yeah, and I'm not sure at what level this could be done or, or that's just going to have to be a continuous assessment."

"Right."

"But if it came down to that, um, uh, it would make life a lot easier all the way around. Because if she was left on the shore—uh, suppose, uh, Newbold decided to go in for some wetwork," Moore ponders.

"Right."

"She was left on the shore she'd be screaming and the FBI would be running around and—it'd be a real mess."

"Really?" Poppa says, as the FBI's tape recorder is running.

"Well, I mean, that's just options within options, within options," Moore concludes.

Moore tells him that after he meets with Newbold Smith, he wants to spend a few days tracking down Galen Kelly. Furthermore, he tells Poppa this work could be potentially lucrative. "Believe it or not, cult work is also relatively well paying. The kids who end up in cults and their parents care about it, have got money. And when it comes to a LaRouche case, frankly my shingle on the door, my name on the door, says it all."

10 | Shoot to Kill

Don Moore is becoming more and more excited, and his talk is sounding more and more violent. He relates a story to Doug Poppa about his efforts to prevent Lyndon LaRouche from having security guards while LaRouche was campaigning for President during the 1988 campaign. Moore says he saw a broadcast on a Washington, D.C. TV station featuring LaRouche, who at the time was being guarded by some off-duty D.C. policemen. Moore tells Poppa how he intervened.

"They suddenly realized that it was on national TV that their guys were guarding this criminal LaRouche. And finally I called them back and I called up the head of I.A. [Internal Affairs], and I said, and he said, 'Well, you know, we don't want to push this thing or the chief doesn't want to push it.' And I said, 'Fine.' I said, 'I'll tell the words I am now going to tell the FBI: Shoot to Kill. Those guys are armed. They have been warned. When the time comes to arrest LaRouche—and I'm a Special U.S. Marshal right now, and I'm telling you, if one of those guys goes for his pocket, when I pull up to arrest him, I am going to start shooting until the screaming stops. And I'm going to tell everybody in D.C. exactly about our conversation.' "

"What did he do?" Poppa asks.

"Well, he just said, 'You have no right.' I said, 'I've got every right in the world.' I mean, I was just berserk. I called him a crud bastard, and as a matter of fact I called his—he sent a black lieutenant out to interview me, I called her a cunt-faced liar, and you know," Moore seethes.

◆ ◆ ◆

His involvement in efforts to kill LaRouche were not limited to the incident he was describing to Poppa. In his first assignment on the LaRouche case in 1985, Moore teamed up with the ADL's Mira Lansky Boland of the Washington ADL office to deny concealed weapons permits for LaRouche's security guards in Loudoun County, Virginia.

LaRouche and his wife, Helga Zepp-LaRouche, had been the target of assassination attempts since the early 1970s. According to U.S. government documents, in 1973, the FBI collaborated with the Communist Party U.S.A. in a plot to "eliminate" LaRouche. In 1977, LaRouche was informed by U.S. intelligence services that he was on the target list of the terrorist Baader-Meinhof gang. Others on that list, banker Juergen Ponto (earlier), and industrialist Hanns-Martin Schleyer (later), were assassinated by the Baader-Meinhof. Later, Helga LaRouche was nearly killed in two vehicular homicide attempts. LaRouche had received repeated death threats from the Jewish Defense League. Repeatedly, from 1983 through 1986, the Soviet government, through featured articles in its leading official press, had called for LaRouche's head.

Based on the obvious need for the LaRouches to have security, the guards had been granted the Virginia concealed weapon permits one year earlier. There had been no change of circumstances to obviate what should have been a routine renewal—except for the fact that the ADL and Moore were hell-bent on setting LaRouche up for assassination.

♦ ♦ ♦

It was in the early morning of October 6, 1986, that the operation to assassinate LaRouche went live. On that day, an assault force of over 400 officers from the FBI, Internal Revenue Service, Secret Service, Bureau of Alcohol, Tobacco and Firearms, Virginia State Police and Loudoun County Sheriff's Department converged on Leesburg, raiding offices of LaRouche's associates under the guise of executing a search warrant. The assault force was equipped with an armored personnel carrier, helicopters, fixed wing aircraft, and other sophisticated weaponry.

At least one of the vehicles used in the raid was provided by ARGUS (Armored Response Group U.S.), the private paramilitary support group founded by Sheriff John Isom and a Virginia millionaire, J.C. Herbert Bryant—the latter the son of a longstanding crony of U.S. District Judge Albert Bryan, Jr., later LaRouche's trial judge in Alexandria.

Embedded within the assault force were specially trained federal and state sharpshooters.

Don Moore was guiding the search teams from building to building throughout town. Mira Lansky Boland herself was lurking around in Leesburg that day.

The raiding party sealed off and searched every office in town that had anything to do with LaRouche. Truckloads of documents were then carted off to a secret military installation.

Simultaneously, an assault force surrounded Ibykus Farm, where Lyndon and Helga LaRouche were staying.

In the late evening of October 6, the assault forces around Ibykus were beefed up and the sharpshooters took up positions. At 10:00 p.m., TV news reporter Jackie Stone broadcast a live report on Washington, D.C.'s Channel 5 from outside Ibykus Farm. Stone reported that authorities were awaiting the imminent arrival of a search warrant and were going to enter the property where there was an "illegal weapons cache."

No such weapons cache existed; and ATF reports later released prove that the authorities knew it. This was only the pretext to launch an assault where the LaRouches would be killed in a hail of gunfire.

With the attack looming, LaRouche fired off a telegram to President Ronald Reagan: "There is no basis for any indictment or arrest of me. I have committed no crime. Any attempted arrest or arrest, would be an attempt to kill me. I will not submit passively to such an arrest, but in such a scenario, I will defend myself. The Reagan administration will go down in ignominy in history, if such a scenario comes to pass."

Shortly after LaRouche sent that message, the attack was called off.

In the days leading up to the raid, there was a flurry of meetings between federal and state officials over who would lead the operation. High-level meetings took place between Virginia's Eastern District U.S. Attorney Henry Hudson and Virginia Attorney General Mary Sue Terry.

According to FBI documents, Terry's insistence on having the State Police be the lead agency "was construed to be for politically motivated reasons."

According to sources close to the investigation, the dispute between the FBI and Terry was over the execution of the assault on LaRouche himself. Moore had proposed a plan for the attack which was initially accepted, then rejected by the feds. Moore then took his plan to the Virginia State Police, who were more enthusiastic. After the Terry-Hudson meetings, the State Police cooled to Moore's proposal. Moore reportedly volunteered to go in alone, claiming he could take out LaRouche himself.

11 | Wetwork

It is 1:00 p.m. on August 17, and Doug Poppa is checking the messages on his answering machine. The first message is from Don Moore: "I plan to leave tomorrow afternoon and go on up to Newbold's and you're welcome to come along, etc. And then from there I'm going further north to South Amboy, etc. and tentatively set up a meeting with Biker Bob, and some interesting people that no matter what you're into, you probably ought to meet. So give me a call and I will try and get back to you in or out of the house, whatever. Take care."

"I got your message. So what's the scoop for tomorrow?" Poppa asks, returning the call.

"We'll try to leave tomorrow afternoon around noonish," Moore says.

"Okay."

"Gotta see Newbold, go from there up to New Jersey where we meet Biker Bob and Carol."

"Right," Poppa responds.

Moore doesn't ask if Poppa had gone to South Amboy for the bikers' barbecue over the weekend as he had planned, and had met Biker Bob. In fact, Poppa hadn't.

"I'll try and set up a meeting with Galen if at all possible," Moore says.

"Right."

"And we'll go from there. Plan to be back by the weekend."

"Okay."

"I don't have any credit—hopefully Newbold will pay me in cash. If that's the case, I'll be flush. But if not, you know, we're going to be sleeping in cars," Moore says.

"Well, we could always, you know, go on the street corner in New York and sit on the grate or something," Poppa teases.

"Doug, in New York, me?" Moore says, laughing under his breath, but sounding like he's taking Poppa's remark more seriously than it was intended. "Not unless I am armed with six different calibers of revolvers. Do you understand?"

"Yes." Poppa is slightly taken aback by Moore's vehemence.

"That motherfucker that comes up and touches me, I'm going off like an ammo dump. It's going to look like Pearl Harbor." Moore is getting worked up.

"All right."

"With no planes in the air."

"All right."

"Ships blowing up. I will shoot anything that moves in New York."

"All right."

"I would shoot a subway train, just because I didn't know what it looks like," says Moore, sounding like he's having a Vietnam flashback.

"Right."

"Unidentified Firing Object, but that's tentatively where it's at," Moore says, with some heat.

Poppa lets the subject drop. Moore says he'll pick him up around noon the next day.

♦ ♦ ♦

On the ride up to Philadelphia, Moore, anxious for Poppa to make a good impression on Newbold Smith and his wife, Peggy, lectures Poppa on manners.

Make sure you use the correct fork when you eat, he says. You're supposed to use the outside fork first, he lectures, giving Poppa other instructions.

Poppa is disgusted at Moore's grovelling. He doesn't intend to propitiate Newbold. He plans to gather evidence of criminal activity.

It is 7:30 p.m. before they arrive at Newbold's mansion. They go into the living room, where Peggy offers them drinks. Newbold appears to have had a few already.

Moore starts right in, telling Newbold and Peggy that Lewis was seen down in Leesburg recently.

"He was down in Leesburg for a couple of days, okay? What had happened was he had come down for some bicycle thing. I didn't know he'd been spotted in town, until finally Doug Graham got ahold of him," Moore said, referring to a photographer for the *Loudoun Times-Mirror*.

"He had said, 'Yeah, my wife had seen him at the bicycle store, he had come in with some complaint about not having cleats for his bike. I didn't even know he was into bikes.'" Moore continues, "I said, you sure we're talking the same person? I brought over a photograph. Same person. Well, she knows because she used to work at the camera store where he used to bring his film. As a matter of fact, the film that he took in Italy."

Doug Graham is a photographer for the *Loudoun Times-Mirror*, the weekly "newspaper of record" in Loudoun County. Graham was friends with the *Times-Mirror*'s former reporter, Bryan Chitwood, who had scribbled so many slanderous articles about LaRouche and his associates. Graham and his wife, Dawn, were also eager members of Moore's underground spy network. Dawn had worked at the Camera Bag, a photography store in Leesburg. Whenever a LaRouche associate brought in film to be developed, she, acting outside the law, without the knowledge or consent of her customer, made an extra set of prints for Moore.

"Do you folks have pictures of the wedding?" Moore asks, touching a raw nerve in Newbold.

"No," Newbold says curtly.

"You don't? I thought I sent you some," Moore says, feeling good that he has something Newbold might want. But Newbold indicates his displeasure with a growl.

"Not that you would want them," Moore backs off. "I mean, your son kneeling at the altar in this old Catholic church with Lyndon LaRouche."

Newbold is grunting with simmering anger as Moore rubs two sore spots in one sentence: Catholics and LaRouche.

"I understand it's a sore subject, because—" Moore hastily says.

"It's a very sore subject, but it doesn't mean anything," Newbold angrily cuts him off.

"Well, anyway I've got these." Moore quickly retreats, as Peggy tries to calm things down.

"Anything new about Galen?" Newbold interrupts,

bringing the discussion around to his main interest, snatching his son, Lewis.

"Yes. I had an appointment for me to go up and see him Wednesday evening."

"Galen is home?" Newbold breaks in expectantly.

"No, no, no, no, Biker Bob Point. We talked in language where once we get to Biker Bob's, I will talk to Galen, whether it's personally or on the phone or whatever."

"Everything's on absolute hold until we get Galen," Newbold insists.

"Well, this is why I've decided to force the issue. I mean, if I have to go see him, I'll go see him," Moore responds. "And I think Bob will cooperate."

"No one knows where Galen is?" Peggy asks, sounding bewildered.

"He didn't want to talk on the phone. Yes, nobody is saying on the phone where Galen is; that's why I'm going to see face to face with Point," Moore explains. "It's not characteristic of Galen whatsoever, and uh, he's not on a mission from God."

"Now, I have my own opinion as to what has happened, and I will reserve that until such time as I confirm or deny it, but I know there has been a problem and we will un-sort it, and we will get Galen back on the wavelength." Moore is being vague, because he knows exactly why Galen is out of touch—the failed May kidnapping in Washington—but he wants to reassure Newbold that everything will still proceed.

"Let's say Galen's out of pocket for whatever reason. It seems to me that for what we want Galen to do he should be out of pocket anyway," Newbold adds, showing an understanding for the unsaid. "By that I mean if I understand what the best—"

"case scenario," Moore completes his sentence.

"—scenario would be to bring Lewis to wherever Galen is, and let Galen perform," Newbold continues.

◆ ◆ ◆

"My problem is this, uh, I have been putting Bobby Greenberg on a sort of quasi-hold," Moore reports on his own angle. "Okay, I've been talking with him, etc., I want to get into some depth, but I want, would like him to be there. Bobby was the last person who dealt with Lewis, and I wanted to do an update where his head is, with Galen alongside. I can do it without him, I've done it before. Most of the people I've brought out—but if I have an option, I'd love to do it with Galen, or at least Galen says 'when you're talking to him, I would like the answers to the following questions.' "

Newbold doesn't understand what Moore is talking about.

Moore begins again. "Okay, I have been talking about Greenberg, but not going into any great depth about Lewis. Other than the cursory, what is and what will be. Before I go into any depth about Lewis with Greenberg, I wanted Galen to be along for the ride, to be there when I ask those questions, because those answers, I feel—" Moore is now thinking out loud.

"Now, I can also, I could, I could tape it if necessary. I can, I could do something along those lines so that Galen could get a feeling for what went on, but if there was a nuance that Bobby brought out, that would maybe be missed by me because I've always been interested in the law enforcement, legal beagle, 'let's lock 'em up' side of the house, as opposed to the psychological 'what shall we do with the mind' kind of thing. You know, I lock up their bodies, their minds will follow. And Galen's situation is more concerned with appearances. And if there was something missing, I would want him to pick up. If you don't want to do it with me, fine; I just want to ask him one question: 'Do you want to do Greenberg with me or not?' "

"What do you mean, 'Do you want to do Greenberg'?" Newbold is perplexed by Moore's ramblings.

"Sit down with Greenberg and spend an afternoon and just go through where they are right now as far as the organization goes. Go out to my place. You can come on out for a barbecue at my place, sit down, and we'll just talk. Where are they on the pathway? You see, the problem is, that we really haven't had an insider feel in the last couple years, and he left because of what went on. See, basically the walls are caving in, people are moving around—"

Peggy recognizes Greenberg's name.

Moore finally explains. He is referring to Bobby and Paul Greenberg, former associates of LaRouche.

"Okay. Paul Greenberg was locked up. His brother in Chicago was locked up in the federal case, went to jail the same day Lyndon LaRouche did, is now out of jail," Moore says. "And I had corresponded with him while he was in jail. Because I had picked up some of these daily briefings that we got out of the trash. There was a point where LaRouche said in the briefing, you know, basically he had been screwed by the Greenbergs and a bunch of other things and that usually that was the same indication

I would get for example, when Zoakos got out and Curtis got out, and the others."

Moore continues, "You would get this tirade by LaRouche against this one ex-member. At that point I said okay, time to come up on the dial. I began to—well, actually I got Zoakos to do an introduction for me. I began to correspond with his brother in jail. His brother wrote me back, surprisingly. I sent him the briefing. We've maintained a cordial, white ear type of relationship. And it's been that way for the past couple months. I've been, I've been—I've not gone into any depth simply because I wanted Galen, okay? Galen."

Moore is referring to former LaRouche associates, whom he now counts as on his side in his "war" against LaRouche. Criton Zoakos was an associate of LaRouche who betrayed his colleagues when he was threatened with deportation for lying to the Immigration and Naturalization Service.

♦ ♦ ♦

But Newbold brings the discussion back to his main concern. "I don't think there is really anything that can be done until you can have somebody who can work on Lewis's head. I think we're absolutely at a dead standstill unless we have Galen Kelly in the wings," Newbold says insistently.

"I would almost agree with you except for one other point, you'd mentioned the Catholic priest," Moore reminds Newbold.

"Yeah, but you know, working through the Catholic Church, who, by the way, are very, very, very anti-LaRouche, is such a long, roundabout, peripheral way of getting the job done, that I think that—Galen and I visited that subject on several occasions, and we always kind of concluded amongst ourselves, I think that, ah, it, it, it raises more problems than it solves," Newbold says, rejecting the idea.

"I still think that the only simple solution to Lewis is somehow to lift Lewis into an association with Galen and riding it out," Newbold insists. "I mean, I don't see what we have to gain. I mean, what the hell can Peggy and I do, without, short of getting ourselves—our tits in a wringer."

"I, I, I don't disagree with you one little bit," Moore acknowledges Newbold's argument. "Number one, we have to get some kind of financial agreement."

"I know." Newbold is willing to pay.

"I need to get something from Galen. Whether it, ah, what are you doing, what are you likely to do, what are you gonna be, you know, and give me a picture for the next six months," Moore says.

"Talk to Point, to Bob Point," Newbold directs.

"Point has assured me that I will be talking to Galen. Now, I suspect that may be on the phone. When you're talking from a lawyer's office nobody had better ever wiretap a lawyer's office," Moore says.

Poppa, listening to this, thinks to himself, that the one exception to that rule is if the lawyer's office is being used in furtherance of a crime.

Moore continues to insist that Newbold must consider targetting Lewis's wife, Andrea, also.

"I guess my point, my dream scenario and it's always been—I've always said that the problems with picking up in any fashion Lewis, is if his wife is still in the organization, and we don't know one way or the other, though she'd be the complaining party. She would be the sorrow on TV or whatever the—you know, they would—Lewis is missing, the family did it, the whole nine yards. Okay, let's say the other end of that scenario, and I don't think anybody ever tested the waters on this. Let's say she wants out of the organization," Moore floats his scenario.

Newbold's listening to this but not paying much attention. He's mainly thinking how to snatch Lewis. "Let me ask you something, um, all ah, purely hypothetical," he interjects. "Supposing Galen was somewhere and uh, he could under certain circumstances could be the bearded—"

"Sage." Moore eagerly completes the sentence, referring to Kelly, who has a beard.

"Sage. This a risk worth taking. Uh, my question is, is it practical to think in terms of lifting him and taking him to Galen, and that, before you answer the question, ah, what I'm saying is, the question doesn't suppose you or Doug or Jo Jo or anybody else you just sent in—is that a practical possibility or is it fraught with such downside risks, that in and of itself, nobody gonna want to do it? Or, down sides or risks to the family. I mean, I don't want to be—as you know, we don't want to be a part of it and shouldn't be—" Newbold wants to maintain his plausible deniability.

"Don't want the knowledge of it," he continues, "but all that I'm saying is, look, somebody's got to get him to Galen, whether it's the Hebraic people from New York that you mentioned, with the long beard and the hat, or whoever it might be, you know. I don't know who it would be, but, or what the pretext would be, whether it's the CIA, you know, all of those sort of formula. I, I'm not even worried about that, and don't even want to worry about it. All I'm saying is, can you conceive of his being lifted and brought to the psychologist who is gonna do it?"

"The answer is the same one that I think we discussed last time," Moore says. "If you are talking about a police action, occurs on the street, no. Fraught with danger, fraught with every peril that you can possibly imagine. Let us say one of several scenarios is that Lewis lends himself to that action, how we discussed, the affair." Moore favors using a woman to lure Lewis.

"Yeah, but even if he has the affair, it's still a pickle," Newbold says.

"Sure, but he has, he has, covered his own tail. We, nobody would be able to cover up when it occurred unless he contributes to his own downfall," Moore explains.

"I see," Newbold acknowledges.

"Whether the downfall is the wife, daughter says, eh, sister says, hey, I've been talking with her, she wants Lewis out, they're going on vacation next week, you know I know. I am her sister, I will be there with you if necessary. Whatever, okay, that's one thing."

"That's a dream," Newbold deflates Moore's plan. "In my opinion," he adds politely.

◆ ◆ ◆

Newbold is getting impatient. He is beginning to realize that if he wants Lewis kidnapped, Moore can't do it alone. "Let me be very specific," he begins. "The last time I talked to Galen, which was sometime earlier this year, my impression was that he could only look to you for intel, not for anything beyond intel, not for any what do you call it?"

"Wetwork," Moore inserts.

"Wetwork," Smith repeats, frustrated. "Because

you've too much at stake to be involved in wetwork, so everybody's got problems with wetwork. Well, intelligence work, I don't minimize that, but all I'm trying to tell you is, look fellahs, look everybody, ah, if, if we're all so spooked out, everybody is goosey, that we don't open our respective persons to what the necessary—God knows, what it'll be now—and ah, multitude of reasons why we wouldn't want to be involved. And at the same time, having said that," Smith says, emboldened, "I know damn well that's what the LaRouchies count on—is our inability to do anything."

They can't do anything without Kelly. "I have done what I can do, you've done what you can. I think everybody's done what they can do. The thing is now, okay, Galen, ah, you know we need some clear thought process," Moore says.

12 | They're on the Edge

Don Moore and Doug Poppa spend the night at the Smith mansion in Radnor, Pennsylvania. Before leaving for South Amboy, New Jersey, and "Biker Bob" Point's office, they have breakfast with Newbold and Peggy Smith. Over English muffins and coffee, Moore and the Smiths vent their extreme hatred for Lyndon LaRouche.

"How old is LaRouche now?" Peggy asks.

"About 70?" Newbold answers tentatively, turning to Moore for confirmation.

"Yes, he's actually—" Moore begins.

"How many more years of jail does he have?" Peggy asks.

"Well, if you're talking realistically he's probably got another three and a half, and I say that because he comes up for parole—I don't think he's going to make the first parole, to answer your question, but I think he'll make it shortly thereafterwards. Simply because he's got a pancreatic problem, which I'm praying is cancer," Moore says with malice, adding, "I hope that, you know, that's the case."

Peggy starts laughing when Moore mentions cancer. "That would be nice," she gloats.

"If that weren't the case, somebody ought to inject him with cancer or something, because he is a cancer," Newbold growls.

Moore tells Peggy their plans for the day. "Well, let's put it this way. I'm going to call Newbold at work later with what we find out up there. Now, it may be they say, Galen is not here, we can't go any further with this. I'm just going to set up a meeting and that's all I'm going to ask over the phone. I'm not about to ask any further. Once I get there, I'll know infinitely more of what I need to know. I will communicate that."

"And you'll be here for supper?" Peggy asks.

"That's what we intend, and that's a 90 percent probability, but if Galen was located with two hours to go, we might make a detour and stick around."

"So if I don't hear from you, you'll be here?"

"Well, Newbold will know by the time he walks in the house what—"

"Yeah, but I'd like to know before," Peggy insists.

"Oh, yes, ma'am, all right. I'll call you at the house or something. All right. That's settled," Moore assures her.

"Okay. All right," Peggy confirms.

"It's really difficult. I've never been able to understand how they get around so many Jewish people," Newbold says, turning the discussion back to the LaRouche movement.

"Jews are highly susceptible to cults," theorizes Moore, one of the ADL's favorite anti-Semites. "It is the one religion, and I will tell you over and over again, there's a book. As a matter of fact, I'll have to order the book and get it to you. It's put out by, as a matter of fact, by the CAN folks, and it is on why the Jewish religion is so susceptible to becoming a cult, entering cults, etc. And if you really look at the difference between, say, Protestant, Catholic and Jewish, you have had a few Protestant cults. You've had a few Catholic cults. But you had multiplicities of Catholic, uh, of Jewish cults. It's partly due to the fact that they practice individualistic, non-group-oriented religion. And, in a sense, yes, they go to the synagogue, but it's not like the Baptists go to raise their hands and have a good time," Moore states.

He continues pontificating. "You know, church is not a social occasion within the Jewish religion. They do the Seder. Everything's done at the table, family, the table. As a result, it lends itself to that conspiratorial thought process."

Newbold, another one of the ADL's favorite anti-Semites, says, "Well, also part of it, I think you're saying, is the fact it's probably—there are only about 15 million in the world, and by persecution over the centuries, starting with Jesus Christ, who was crucified by Jews, and the Christians held that against the Jews, I suppose. In any way, the Jews are forced to get, and they retreated into that perimeter, quote, unquote, and the perimeter translates, I think that a lot of their mentality is defensive mentality against forces that might wipe them out, or something."

He goes on, "I don't think any religion, whether it's Jew or Roman Catholic, Episcopalian, Presbyterian, or any other sects, have a monopoly on cults or have a monopoly on strange behavior."

Moore responds, "I have no personal experience other than the LaRouche organization. I have to tell you that none of these have a higher percentage of Jews, and they are hard to get out. Greenberg is the first Jew that I'm aware of that came out," Moore says, referring to Bobby Greenberg.

"Really?" Newbold exclaims.

"Yes, I can't think of any others. Chris Curtis was not Jewish. And Zoakos got out because he was Catholic. Tate got out not for any religious reason whatsoever. Mandel, I'm trying to think of some other people I know. Not one that has any Jewish thing whatsoever. They were all either Catholic—" Moore ticks off a list of former LaRouche associates.

"I'll tell you one thing about Jews. They can talk about themselves and talk about Zionism, and all the rest of it, and other Jews, much more objectively than certain other religions can," Newbold interjects.

♦ ♦ ♦

After breakfast, Moore and Poppa leave for South Amboy to meet lawyer Bob Point and, Moore hopes, Galen Kelly. When they arrive, Point tells them that Kelly is still hiding out, and that there are indications that the FBI is investigating Kelly.

Moore reminds Point that the last time they talked, Kelly "was dealing with Tony Russo up in New York and had some problems with a thing that had gone sour before, involving this gal that was like a prostitute."

♦ ♦ ♦

Moore was referring to yet another kidnapping. On September 17, 1991, Galen Kelly and several other men abducted a woman in New York City. They were hired by the woman's parents, who wanted the woman "deprogrammed" from her boyfriend. At around noon, Kelly's team knocked on the woman's door, posing as police carrying out a drug bust. They told the woman they were taking her down to the police station and they carried her off to a waiting van. The woman was driven to a cabin in Pennsylvania, where she was taken into a bedroom and held down on the bed.

Screaming, the woman demanded to be set free, accusing the men of kidnapping her. Galen Kelly said, "I've heard it before. They all say it. The fact is, you're here." The woman repeatedly demanded to be released, promising to prosecute Kelly and his accomplices for kidnapping. Every time she said this, Kelly told her this kind of kidnapping had gone to court before, and no one had ever been convicted. He told her that her parents were coming and that they wanted to give her some information she needed to know.

The woman was held in the cabin for three days, until, on September 20, she was taken to a house in upstate New York, believed to be the home of Tony Russo, who lived in Newburgh.

Three days later, on September 23, a rabbi named Tsvi Kilstein, believed to be a member of the terrorist Jewish Defense League, arrived at the house with some of CAN's anti-cult videos and literature. The woman was told she would be freed after she watched the videos and read the literature. The abductors told her they wanted to take her to Wellsprings clinic in Ohio for counseling. When the woman refused, they said they would take her to a counselor in New Jersey. Thinking she could escape during the trip, the woman agreed.

Once in New Jersey she was held in a house for three more days, until September 26. At that point, the woman persuaded Rabbi Kilstein to release her. Kilstein took her to a meeting in Elizabeth, New Jersey with Galen Kelly. Upset that the deprogramming had not worked, Kelly tried to persuade the woman not to go back to New York. She insisted, and later that afternoon, Kilstein drove her back to New York City, dropping her off at the Salvation Army.

The next day, the woman made a report to the FBI, which opened an active investigation into the kidnapping.

◆ ◆ ◆

Now, Point tells Moore that Kelly may make contact with him, so Moore proposes an arrangement to set up a meeting. He says that Newbold has a place in South Philadelphia where they can meet. "You've got your Galen, bring him on down there. I know Newbold wants to talk to him, we can drive down and pick him up. And spend a couple of days down there, you know, staring at the ceiling, talking, maybe talking, moving over." Moore is trying to be circumspect.

At 3:30 p.m. Poppa speaks into his hidden microphone, hoping the FBI can hear. He tells them they will be leaving Point's soon and that Point called Kelly's wife, Liz, and left a message for Kelly to call Newbold.

The two men then head back to Newbold's mansion, where they plan to spend the night.

"Well, we'll know something tonight. Whether he's in or out." Poppa wonders out loud if Kelly will ever surface, saying, "Doesn't sound good, though."

"I agree," Moore says.

"Well, maybe that's what he needs. Maybe he needs a kick in the butt and say, hey, get back into life and start uh, working again," Poppa says.

Moore agrees. "The thing is, that this guy has been in the front lines for 20 years. He was one of the first deprogrammers. He was the guy that basically sort of developed, if you want to call it, snatching, or you want to call it kidnapping or deprogramming, you know, pick your own vocabulary. But he was the guy that was the front line character."

"Right."

◆ ◆ ◆

As they turn onto the New Jersey Turnpike, Moore tells Poppa what he knows about Kelly's past kidnappings. "This pimp had several girls working for him, and now she's divorced. So the family wanted her back and the pimp said, 'Hey I got a good thing going.' Galen ended up just kicking the fucking door down, tied this guy up and took the girl. So anyway, the guy calls the feds and the feds start looking into it. They call up Galen. Galen says, 'Oh, you know, just before you get too far here, you know, you need to understand the character of the man that you've just been involved with.' 'What do you mean?' 'You know, pimp.' 'Oh?' 'Yeah, um, sorry, nobody makes any representations that we're saving a girl from a life of crime.' Which is what you're supposed to do if you're a law man. Well, they went back, checked it out, and said, 'Never mind,' and that was the end of it."

On the New Jersey Turnpike, Moore's car blows a head gasket. While waiting for the repairs, Moore talks about the D.C. kidnapping from May 1992. "And you know, this one week Galen made a mistake, I said, hey, put you on target there at the Chrysler as you go get her, and somebody, a different girl took the car. They followed the car, didn't even check the pictures I had. Snatching's—everything's fine."

"Right," Poppa says.

"Wrong person. Anyway, they want to find out who this other girl is, right?"

"Right."

"This girl says, 'I'll never talk, I'll never tell you.' So the woman goes, 'Give me a half an hour. She will talk. Where are my knitting needles?' Ha, ha, ha, ha, ha, ha," Moore laughs gleefully. "Yeah, Galen's going, 'Wait a minute.' He's thinking this is a do-over. 'We can cut her loose and forget.' 'I can make her talk, I guarantee you she will talk.' Galen thinks, 'Where is she going to put those knitting needles?' "

"So these two people are?" Poppa asks, referring to the woman with the knitting needles, and the kidnap victim.

"Lubavitch," Moore answers, referring to the woman with the needles.

"Lubavitch," Poppa repeats.

Moore shows Poppa pictures of the girl he and Kelly kidnapped. Poppa has been told about the D.C. kidnapping by the FBI, but this was the first time Moore had ever told him of his personal involvement.

Moore explains, "There is an entire subculture of people like Bob Point, people like Galen Kelly, people like Carol, who are not spies, they're not CIA agents, they're not arms dealers. They're a set of guys who hang out with the guys that do. They're on the edge, they're on the periphery of it, and sometimes they become a major player and sometimes they don't."

◀ Pat Lynch, shown in 1984 outside LaRouche's Loudoun County residence, while she was preparing the slanderous NBC-TV "First Camera" show on LaRouche. Lynch, who now works for CBS, was in the cheering section for the recent Kidnappers, Inc. trial.

EIRNS

▶ Washington, D.C. ADL fact-finding director Mira Lansky Boland, during the Kidnappers, Inc. trial. Boland is an integral part of the Get LaRouche strike force, and a controller of Don Moore.

EIRNS/Stuart Lewis

Transmit the following in _____
_____(Type in plaintext or code)_____

Via AIRTEL _____
_____(Priority)_____

TO: DIRECTOR, FBI (100-392623)

FROM: SAC, NEW YORK (100-123674) (P)

SUBJECT: LYNDON HERMYLE LA ROUCHE JR., aka
Lynn Marcus
SM-NCLC
(OO:NY)

ReBulet, 10/29/73.

In reviewing New York case file it is noted that information has been received that the CPUSA is conducting an extensive background investigation on the subject for the purpose of ultimately eliminating him and the threat of the NCLC, on CP operations. Several sources have furnished this information to the New York office, and this information has appeared in the Daily World newspaper several times.

NCLC sources have advised that the subject is the controlling force behind the NCLC and all of its activities. A discussion with the New York NCLC case agent indicates that it is felt if the subject was no longer in control of NCLC operations that the NCLC would fall apart with internal strife and conflict.

New York proposes submitting a blind memorandum to the "Daily World" CP newspaper, in New York City which has been mailed from outside this area to help facilitate CP investigations on the subject. It is felt that this would be appropriate under the Bureau's counter intelligence program.

The blind memorandum is enclosed. 100-392623-45

Bureau comments are requested on such a proposal. 15 NOV 1973

EX-110

②- Bureau (RM) (Encl. 2)
1 - New York

1977

Approved _____ Sent _____ M Per _____
Special Agent in Charge

U.S. Government Printing Office: 1972 —

A 1973 FBI Cointelpro document (obtained under the Freedom of Information Act) confirms that the FBI was planning to use the Communist Party U.S.A. to eliminate LaRouche.

◄ Among those who wanted to see LaRouche prosecuted was Iran-Contra conspirator Oliver North, Don Moore's Vietnam tentmate.

▼ The telegram from Iran-Contra's Gen. Richard Secord to Oliver North that surfaced during the Boston LaRouche trial, indicating that North regarded LaRouche as a threat to his operations.

EIRNS/Stuart Lewis

Copp: 5/5/86 1150

051625Z May 86. Our source reports that terrorists plan to use airfield near Texas border. Strip is at intersection of Marfa vor 280 radial and Hudspeth vor 168 radial. Lewis has met with FBI and other agency reps and is apparently meeting again today. Our man here claims Lewis has collected info against Larouche -- let's see how polygraph goes. Rgds, Dick. BT

▲ Then-U.S. Attorney for Virginia's Eastern District Henry Hudson (left) with Justice Dept. lawyer Mark Rasch, at an Oct. 14, 1988 press conference in Alexandria announcing the indictment of Lyndon LaRouche and six of his associates, after the Boston federal prosecution failed because of government misconduct.

▶ Politically ambitious Virginia Attorney General Mary Sue Terry went after LaRouche associates to further her career.

► Virginia Senior Assistant Attorney General John Russell, who lied for Don Moore in the Kidnappers, Inc. trial to protect the Virginia LaRouche cases, for which he has been lead prosecutor.

▼ Then-assistant U.S. Attorney John Markham, shown after Lyndon LaRouche was given an effective life sentence in January 1989.

EIRNS/Philip Ulanowsky

EIRNS/Stuart Lewis

EIRNS/Stuart Lewis

As Loudoun County Sheriff's Deputies and Virginia State Police stand guard, FBI agents load thousands of documents into a truck during the Oct. 6-7, 1986 raid on offices of LaRouche's associates in Leesburg, Va.

An armored personnel carrier used in the Oct. 1986 raid belonged to ARGUS, a paramilitary group founded by Loudoun County, Va. Sheriff John Isom (shown left, below) with ARGUS's head, J.C. Herbert Bryant.

EIRNS/Stuart Lewis

EIRNS/Carlos De Hoyos

Don Moore's house near Lovettsville, Va. In the garage can be seen some of the filing cabinets where Moore kept the files from a seven-year-long investigation of LaRouche while Moore was a Loudoun Sheriff's Deputy. Inset: Moore in uniform. He was fired in March 1992, reportedly for rifling Sheriff John Isom's files.

EIRNS/Stuart Lewis

13 | Galen Is Back

After again spending the night at Newbold Smith's house in Radnor, Don Moore and Doug Poppa pick up Moore's car and head back to Leesburg.

The next day, Poppa goes over to Moore's house to talk. Things are starting to pick up steam. Moore reports that he talked to "Biker Bob" Point, who told him that Galen Kelly had made contact.

While Poppa is in the room, Moore calls Point. Poppa overhears him saying, "Newbold wants to drive up with me, up to either your neck of the woods or Galen's, and have a contract of which he is willing to ah, retain your professional services. He needs to test the real-world reactions to any solutions that he may pose to you. You know, involving snatch and grab, and things like that. And I don't think we advocate that, but, uh—" Moore stops talking and listens to Point, then continues. "Exactly. Uh, that's—why should we retain lawyers when they can tell us that? Right, ha, ha, ha, ha, ha. Yeah, we need to have a hypothetical brainstorming session to answer the rhetorical what ifs. Yes, excellent, the problem with his current attorney," Moore says, referring to the Smith family retainer, David Foulke, "is the guy can't stop coughing when you suggest something like that—he usually requires water and CPR."

Moore pauses again as Point talks. Poppa hears, "Um, and Galen needs to be there, and frankly, you know, so I am looking for a wide, wide world, uh, U.N. meeting, some time and he is off on his boat."

Moore proposes a meeting in mid-September.

Hanging up the phone, Moore turns to Poppa. "You know, part of the problem with the deprogramming is, it comes down to at some point doin' a snatch."

"Right."

"And you and I aren't gonna get involved in that."

"Right."

"But there's nothing to say that we can't, you know, point the finger, and this is where they are, and this is what we do. Da, da, da, da, da, and, and, et cetera, ah, and having said that, you know, we go forth and, and try our best."

"Right."

"Galen brings in a couple of Jewish people, and you and I leave the room and go outside. So I don't have a problem with that myself. Uh, believe it or not, I still think you're doing God's work even though it's quasi, quasi, if you know what I'm saying," Moore justifies the planned kidnapping.

"Right."

"It gets real close to the edge; we're not going over the edge. If Bob's going over the edge, and or Galen might go over the edge, he's not gonna do it with us around and he knows that."

"Right."

"When he gives me a wink, I leave the room and whatever happens, happens," Moore says.

"What happens if by some chance they did the snatch on Lewis or something, and the shit hits the fan?" Poppa asks.

Moore has his alibi ready. "Newbold, for various reasons, is very concerned about what his son is engaged in. And all I'm doing, I didn't engage him in kidnapping or anything else. I did the investigative work that would be done on an individual engaged in criminal activity. The second thing, uh, that would be said was, and it would be very clear demarcation. If something was gonna happen, we go home. We do not answer the phone. We're just not even on the horizon, okay? And if the demarcation is very clear, it's not like we're waiting down the street when something happens. We're not gonna be lookouts, we're not gonna be torpedoes. We're gonna be anything else. We are gonna be back in Loudoun County, with you doing a DJ job."

"When everything goes down?" Poppa asks.

"When everything goes down," Moore assures him.

"What I'm saying is, if the shit ever hits the fan," Poppa starts to ask again.

"It's already hit it twice with these guys," Moore interrupts.

"And they've covered their tracks?" Poppa asks

"They've covered their tracks," Moore again assures him.

◆ ◆ ◆

Four days pass before Poppa gets a call from Moore on August 25.

"What's up?" Poppa asks.

"Number one, Galen is back," Moore says excitedly. "Newbold is going to be calling me at ten, wants to put together a deal. I just wanted you available."

At noon Moore calls back. "I talked to Newbold. Uh, he's gonna send me down two thousand—he was trying to set up a meeting and he will contact me back."

"Do you still want Galen in?" Poppa asks.

"Uh, he's, he, he's in the process of deciding that." Moore tells Poppa to be ready to attend a meeting during the first or second week of September.

Two days later, on August 27, Poppa calls Moore to ask when the meeting will be.

"I think it's gonna be the first week in September. And I'd better get a check in the next couple of days," Moore says.

"Well, he hasn't sent you the check yet?"

"Hasn't sent me a check," Moore answers. "I caught him just after his boat, and I unloaded for a second, I think. I honestly have to believe I don't think he's necessarily stiffing me. This is a guy honestly does not understand the working man. It's almost like he's asking well, why don't you spend your trust fund? And Newbold to earth, Newbold to earth, come in please. You know, most of us don't have trust funds that pay for these kinds of things."

"He thinks everybody's got money," Poppa puts in.

"Yeah, well, and so as a result, uh, the maid was the one to first clue me in on that—Ramona, who I think is in love with you."

"You think so?" Poppa is incredulous.

"Yeah, she wants to have your child," Moore chuckles.

"Did, uh, Galen ever call you up or is this thing—" Poppa starts to ask.

"No, Galen hasn't called at all. And, you know, frankly, I don't care one way or the other."

"Right."

"Frankly, I come with credentials of my own. I'm known throughout the cult network as the guy who put away LaRouche," Moore brags.

Poppa decides to take a vacation for a few days while waiting for the meeting to take place in New Jersey. On September 8, he calls Moore. "I just got in at five this morning," he begins.

"Well, you know, 25 words or less, we're going to meet probably the beginning of next week up there in New Jersey. We'll stay at Newbold's place. I talked to Newbold. Newbold's going to Italy."

"When's he going?" Poppa asks.

"He's going this Thursday."

"Oh, is he really?"

"Yeah, for two weeks. And you know, they just decided to do Italy."

"How are we going to have a meeting with him next week if he's going to Italy?" Poppa asks.

"Well Newbold won't be there. We'll have a meeting with Bob Point and Galen, etc. What I'm going to do is replicate the New Jersey trip and then stay up at Newbold's place. I'm just going to bill him directly for your services."

"All right," Poppa says, then asks, "so how come he doesn't want to be at the meeting? I thought this was a big thing or something."

"Well, he was going to do it himself, and then Bob, who is the attorney, said, one of the ways that you can avoid problems is if we have a meeting and you're in Italy. Then nobody can say there was a conspiracy," Moore reports. "So I mean, that's apparently the thinking that went into it. I'm not going to quibble with anything Bob says, he's an attorney and you know, under the circumstances—that's the best advice available. So it's going to be a world-wide meeting, but it's also going to be a meeting of the East Coast Anti-Cult Attack Force."

14 | A Proposal That's 80 Percent Complete

September 16 comes. Don Moore, Galen Kelly, and Bob Point finally get together at Point's office in New Jersey. Doug Poppa is there with his tape recorder and a hidden transmitter, which broadcasts to a concealed team of FBI agents watching from outside.

As they sit down, Moore shows Kelly some surveillance photos he took of Lewis's new house in Chestnut Hill, in Philadelphia. Mixed in with the surveillance photos are pictures Moore took of Oliver North when they were in Vietnam.

"You'll recognize the guy on the side—there's Oliver North, all right," Moore says.

"You see what a younger Don Moore looks like," comments Kelly.

"This was another shot that I got credit for—the caption says—'I was three sheets to the wind when I found Ollie, 'cause that's who I am, Don Moore.' This shot got taken at the base of the DMZ. Yeah, and he was tanked out on beer as were we all, and I was already coming back. That's just a little itty bit of history there,"

Moore says with relish, passing around other photos. "That's Ollie passed out—I took that shot."

Moore then reports to Kelly the results of his surveillance work, and his contacts with Paul and Bobby Greenberg, former LaRouche associates. Kelly is very interested. Moore wants to set up a meeting with Bobby Greenberg and Kelly, but Greenberg has told Moore he doesn't trust Kelly. When Greenberg was still an associate of LaRouche, he had investigated Kelly, so he knew Kelly was a kidnapper.

"Okay, I brought enough shit. I've brought stuff I've taken out of the trash showing income, showing how it links up computerwise with the disbursement of funds, with the various organizations." Moore shows off his booty on the LaRouche movement, obtained through his favorite investigative method: rooting through other people's garbage.

"They never—" Kelly is amazed.

"They're fucking idiots," Moore says, pulling out a stack of computer sheets. "And a bunch of other computer shit that comes out of their trash. Intercompany transfers of money—you know where the money goes and how it goes out, etc.—Those guys."

Moore had always prided himself for skulking and snooping around the offices of LaRouche's associates in Leesburg. He once testified in court that he used to hide behind bushes outside the Leesburg office buildings where they worked, and hid behind the potted plants where they banked. During one of these surveillance periods, he noticed and made much of LaRouche's associates going to a local butcher shop to buy "prime cuts of beef."

"If they were a country, I'd fucking own 'em, okay?

But that's because I'd be illegal, and I'd just walk in one night with guns and shoot the appropriate people and say, I'm the boss, and everybody would say, okay, he's the boss," Moore says with relish.

"Well, there might be a couple of arrests out there?" Kelly queries, referring to Moore's report on his discussions with Rick Munson of the Minnesota Attorney General's office.

"Yeah, that's what I'm saying. There's at least one arrest at Upper Darby. Two arrests in Chicago. And I'd put them on the Chicago P.D. guys that I dealt with before, when, you remember, there were two LaRouchies who'd won presidential elections out there," Moore confirms, referring to the 1986 Illinois Democratic primary victories of LaRouche-associated candidates Mark Fairchild for lieutenant governor and Janice Hart for Illinois secretary of state, which resulted in Adlai Stevenson III withdrawing as the Democratic candidate for governor.

"I'd gone to Chicago in late '85. And I went to the Chicago police office, which just happened to be the same building where they filmed the opening scenes from Hill Street Blues—when the cruiser comes up and goes—. It's the old Seventh District office, but it's now been pretty well burned out of the area. I stuck my butt out there to lay on them the fact that they got a serious problem because we found stuff in Leesburg showing that Chicago is the next place," Moore brags.

"They blow me off. Some fucking, you know, cornhog deputy from Lowdown County," he goes on. "About six weeks later, was when they win the election in Chicago and blow out Stevenson, I tell you these guys were willing to suck my dick over the phone just to get any information I'd give them. So I dole it out, but I also take stuff from them. And those are the people I put Minnesota in touch with," Moore boasts.

♦ ♦ ♦

Kelly, meanwhile, is trying to figure out an explanation for why Lewis Smith would have purchased such a large house in Philadelphia. "Helga coming to the United States?" he asks, referring to LaRouche's wife, Helga Zepp-LaRouche.

"No. Well, she's not going to come because I have taken great pains to pass rumors amongst those that are European-oriented that Donny Moore has a piece of paper for Helga when she comes, okay? They don't know what that paper is. It might be, you know, have Don call me if he was free, but they think it's a warrant. And I've never disabused them of that," Moore puffs himself.

Kelly pumps Moore for all the latest news about LaRouche and his associates. "How broke are the La-Rouchies? Are they into anything particularly with South Africa? I mean, they got any good informational connections, do you think?"

"Uh, most of the overseas areas is breaking up. And it wouldn't affect Upper Darby anyway," Moore says.

"The South African operations are run from the U.S.," Kelly remarks.

"Yeah that's what I'm saying. And that was run through a guy named DeGroot. But the name of the game is the ones they were backing, is the South African, is backing the white government to track quote ANC members in the United States. And the idea in the LaRouchie philosophy was the ANC members were communists. Therefore, it was easy to swallow, for those who have darker skin in the organization. All the people they backed are gone—Marcos, Noriega. Venezuela's out. I haven't gotten an *EIR* magazine recently, but you know, I think that Bobby can certainly help us on the international situation. What I'm recommending, and you know, New-bold—"

"Anything in Central America?" Kelly interrupts Moore.

"Well if you've been kicked out of Venezuela and Panama they're gonna have real problems anywhere else. They certainly are not going to be in Peru. They backed García up the wazoo and García's crashed. Everybody they've backed is gone," Moore continues.

"Anything with the Iraqis?" Kelly continues probing.

"Yeah, they did a lot with Iraq," Moore says.

"So you know, for years, we always hear that LaRouche people are hurting for money, but they always seem to survive," Kelly says.

"Well, it's because they're like Japanese soldiers, they can live on a bag of rice all day," Moore answers.

Soon the conversation turns back to planning the actual implementation of the kidnapping of Lewis Smith.

◆ ◆ ◆

"My problem," Moore says, "is if, let's say that occurs. Let's say that in scenario number óne he goes to a house. And he's been happy there a few more times in the past, and out there he's relaxed. He takes a drink, falls asleep, ends up as part of a carpet. So we get a van, ends up someplace. And I advocate anything from taking New-bold's ship out to sea beyond the three-mile limit or the twelve-mile limit, or whatever, and spend a couple of weeks cruising the coast while discussions were held." Point shakes his head, no.

"You don't like that," Moore backs off. "Oh, all right."

"You're going to get nailed as a drug boat," Point advises.

"If you never went anywhere, you can't then, you know—?" Moore says.

"The Coast Guard will hammer you in a minute," Point explains.

"All right, okay."

"You got to go where bribery is uh, king." Point offers his legal expertise.

"The land of opportunity and leaving heading south as opposed to heading north," says Kelly.

"My concern was that if the wife was left standing on the shore, in any fashion whatsoever, without having been taken too—" Moore puts in.

"Yeah, so we need to know where the wife stands," Kelly agrees.

"And in one sense or another, make some—" Moore begins to say.

"Accommodations for the wife, whatever accommodation that may be," Kelly finishes the sentence.

"Exactly, cabin for two or whatever," Moore puts in.

"All right, I think, um, I think it's correct. If it was a real—I, I like the female seduction mode, uh, but after that if it was a real paramilitary type of thing, he would think it's an agency plot, and, uh—" Kelly proposes, thinking out loud.

"I think it's gotta be structured down to the little black costumes and the, the whole fuckin'—" Point gives more advice.

"Yeah," Kelly agrees.

"—thing, and you gotta do the MP-5 routine, you gotta, you know what I mean, just ah, say, well, I ain't gonna fuck with these guys," Point completes his thought.

"You've gotta have absolutely overwhelming. He doesn't want to get dead," Kelly says.

"Um hum," Moore agrees.

"Now that's for sure," Kelly continues. "He's a fighter, he's a street fighter, oddly enough. He's a barroom fighter, an airport fighter," Kelly describes Lewis Smith, adding, "but you know, you get five—"

"Plus there's a psychological thing that, uh, like this is bigger than I am." Point interrupts with more lawyerly advice.

"Yeah," Kelly agrees.

"You'll, you'll get in a pissing contest with anybody one on one, two on one, but when it seems organized," Point continues. "And that's real, ingrained that you're going to submit to a perceived authority there and I don't give a fuck who you are."

"So you may, you may lure him into a compromising situation through a female seduction, but then you've got to have the SAS there or something. And off he goes to someplace where bribery is king. And it's gotta be, uh, maybe we can talk him out of this. Would be an incredible challenge. It really would be a challenge. It could be done. But let's assume that it wasn't done. Could we all bow out gracefully?" Kelly ponders.

"You mean if it goes sour?" Moore asks.

"Yeah, bow out gracefully, and I think that contingency would have to be in there. Look, it's not the same thing, but on the other hand, uh, no lack of preparation taken when I snatched that little girl out of Washington. We put her back and nothing happened, because she thought something else and she was afraid of something else. Well, no, she had a good job, but I mean if she had got kidnapped on the street, I mean that had nothing to do with her job. Nah, there were problems there that she was hiding and she was afraid would be revealed," Kelly says, justifying his actions in the May D.C kidnapping.

"Well, that's why I say to a certain extent whoever the young lady was under normal circumstances would be pro forma, understood, that there may well be more than just handshakes involved, and, any—perhaps even a tape or two. Do you understand what I'm saying?" Moore is putting his perverse mind to work. He wants to discuss the details of what Kelly calls the "female seduction mode."

"Okay, what I'm simply saying is even, even, even, if we say a film is delivered and, uh, this is you and the x, y, z, you know, you need to seriously consider your options. Because a threat is no good unless you perceive it as a threat," Moore says.

"Yeah," Kelly agrees.

"I mean, it has to be, it's not a question if we got tapes, it's hey, in the course of, let's take a look at you in the missionary position, or otherwise. And then—" Moore conjectures.

"Or getting tickled with a feather." More lawyering from Point.

"Yeah, right. Right, with a dog collar," Moore says.

"I'm not suggesting this as, as—'cause frankly, re-gardless of what my domestic situation, conflict, is or isn't, I mean over the years, if somebody, I'm not saying that they would have ever had the opportunity, but, hypo-thetically if somebody came home with a videotape, and they said we're going to show this to your wife, or give us the secrets of the world, what can you do? So, tapes in themselves don't necessarily win. But if you get the dog collar," Kelly says, musing over the idea of blackmailing Lewis.

"That's, that's it. You've got to get the, uh, one wild night there," Point advises.

"Listen, I, I was going to say, if you go to bed with a woman and wake up with two guys, I mean, just remember that too," Moore proposes.

"He may have a proclivity for that anyway," Kelly says.

"Well, see now, that would be the other one, I mean it would be the real fuck about this, that you get yourself a nice, ah, he-she," Point interjects.

"But if you know if the unfortunate incident occurs, who else kidnapped somebody two blocks from the White House, and put them back?" Kelly boasts, then goes on. "So, what do we do from here? What do we do? What's Newbold's whereabouts?"

"He'll be back in a week or two. He'll actually be back in the middle of next week," Moore answers.

They resolve that Kelly will come to Leesburg to meet with Bobby Greenberg to determine if he has any information that will be helpful. Kelly also thinks most of the work to prepare for kidnapping Lewis Smith is done. "As a proposal which is 80 percent of it, 90 percent of it, I could bring with me, and the last 10 percent or 20 percent which is A, part of a result of what he has to say; and B, financial considerations which need to be worked out, can be attached," Kelly concludes.

Kelly says that then he can present the final proposal to Newbold.

15 | Sneakers Up in a Ditch

Galen Kelly arrives in Leesburg, Virginia on the evening of Tuesday, September 29, 1992. By then, Don Moore has already had a meeting with Paul and Bobby Greenberg at a Thai restaurant in Falls Church, Virginia. Moore believes the Greenbergs want to get back at LaRouche. He thinks they will cooperate, but he wants them to meet Kelly, something they are reluctant to do.

At 10:05 p.m., Poppa tells his tape recorder, "We left Payne's. We're over at Giovanni's Pizza. While we were in Payne's, Galen talked about some snatching or kidnapping they did in New York City where they kicked in the door. They tied the guy up with an electrical cord and took the girl out. They identified themselves as FBI agents to get into the house and something about a dog was in there, and they were going to take the dog or something. He also said that a guy from the—an ex-NYPD cop named Eddie Sullivan has worked for him in the past. Also, he told me he has in his car right now, and the tag number as I can remember is N.Y. KYX8A8. It looks like an unmarked cruiser with a spotlight. In the trunk of the car

119

he's got an NYPD uniform and an NYPD badge. He identified himself as an NYPD cop when they did the kidnapping of Ann Kleinhurst. They went to the—excuse me, they went to the Wells Fargo office in Falls Church, him and somebody else, and identified themselves as NYPD officers to get information on something about Ann Kleindienst."

Kelly, Moore and Poppa order a pizza and some beers at a Leesburg restaurant. At 10:45 p.m., Poppa leaves another message on his tape: "We're still in Giovanni's. One thing I didn't mention: When we were in Payne's bar, he did not go to Newbold's yet, because he told me and Don, they brought it up. He said I guess that's because we've got to come up with a plan tomorrow. So they don't have any plan right now. We're still in Giovanni's and they're talking about a bunch of nonsense. I'm going to go flip the tape over at this time."

At 11:06 Poppa leaves his last message of the night on his tape recorder. "They just dropped me off in front of Payne's. I'm picking up my car. Don's in Galen's car. Galen's going to drop him off in front of the *Times-Mirror* where Don's car is. Galen's staying over at Don's tonight. The plan is right now I'm supposed to call him up about 10:00. We'll go up to his house and we're laying out the plan so Galen can drop it off to Newbold tomorrow. I'm turning off the machine at this time."

♦ ♦ ♦

The next day, September 30, the weekly issue of the *Loudoun Times-Mirror* hits the street with a front-page story planted by Moore. Headlined "LaRouche Devotee Slapped With Lawsuit," the article reports on Cult Awareness Network head Cynthia Kisser's libel suit against the publishers of *New Federalist* newspaper. The lawsuit's papers have not yet been served, however. Moore has given copies of the suit to Poppa, who has never served them on the defendants.

In the late morning, Poppa meets Moore and Kelly at Moore's house, in the country near Lovettsville, Virginia.

"Is the money good in doing deprogramming stuff?" Poppa asks Kelly.

"Oh, yeah. It's survivable," Kelly replies.

"What happens when something goes wrong? How do you keep from exposing yourself to danger—or not danger I'm talking about, you know, somebody gets locked up someplace?" Poppa asks.

"Well, you have two things. You've got criminal and you've got civil," Kelly says. "The only time you have a criminal problem or any legal problem is if it doesn't work. Where might it not work? It might not work when you're talking about these involuntary deprogrammings." But, he continues, speaking from experience, if you do "your damage control correctly, it's marginal."

"What about this thing with Newbold, is he gonna pay us, for us going up the last time, or that's in the wind, or what are we doing with him?" Poppa asks.

"I don't know where Newbold is, and that's kind of where we are at this point. I mean, Newbold sort of went into a holding pattern. I did what was necessary to keep the temperature warm on the fire, uh, but basically we're doing it on our own," Moore says.

"What Newbold wants to do is, he wants the ultimate solution. He wants—" Kelly says.

"He wants the snatch," Moore completes the sentence.

"Yeah," Kelly agrees.

"It's a big guy," Poppa says.

Kelly proposes using bikers to do the kidnapping.

"What's the advantage of using them over, uh, what you normally use?" Poppa asks.

"I would like to divorce myself. I'd like to find Lewis in some safe and secure place." Kelly says that what he wants is, "Look here's the deal, you go get this guy and deliver him to such and such a place and let me know. And, uh, have no part in the conspiracy. So I would like to just simply contract it out and no, have no role in it, no management, uh, involvement in it whatsoever."

"Right." Poppa says.

"Now, we need people that have an organization. And I think the biker crowd has such an organization, no doubt. And uh, I think they'd be difficult to prosecute. I think they'd be difficult to get a handle on. They all look alike. They disappear. They don't talk. Like organized crime. I mean, they'll drive you crazy," Kelly says. "The other thing would be if I was in touch apparently, which I'm not, with some military want-to-bes of a skill."

"Those soldier of fortune people?" Poppa asks, referring to mercenary soldier types.

"England had the SAS and they could be talented guys, and they have a limited amount of experience, more the last couple of years, than usual. But they want to do something, they're all dressed up," Kelly says.

"All dressed up and no place to go," Moore adds.

"Maybe there were guys that wanted the glamor and excitement. Maybe it's time to direct the *Soldier of Fortune* magazine," Kelly proposes.

"*Soldier of Fortune* thing, I mean, now they're starting to monitor those ads," Moore says.

"Right," Kelly acknowledges.

"After they kill them," Moore finishes.

"I'm afraid of that, but if I could find a power military operation, someplace. So, I really don't want to kidnap Lewis myself, I think it's a mistake, uh, I think it's a lot of problems. It might just work though, so if it might just work, and I think Newbold's entitled to a shot at it, if he can get some people that have the talent. I'd like to contract it out and say, you guys do it," Kelly says.

Moore puts in, "I can't obviously, in my situation, at least right now, end up with somebody pointing a finger at me. The situation is quite frankly such that I have a more than reasonable chance of getting elected. And if that's the case, we may be able to revisit," Moore says, referring to his hopes to become the Loudoun County Sheriff.

Kelly then says, "Let me tell you one of the things I wanted to come to some kind of terms with the Newbold thing. And that is," Kelly says, quoting Smith, " 'I want to go out and kidnap my son.' "

"I couldn't get Newbold to agree on anything." Moore expresses his frustration.

But Kelly is not worried. "I think we're in agreement as to what Newbold wants."

"Yes," Moore agrees.

"Therefore, if I was in England or travelling these days, and knew some SAS guys, I would talk to them. I'm afraid of the soldier of fortune both on a confidence level and uh, getting stung. Bikers are a different story," Kelly says.

"Mmm-hmm," Moore agrees.

Kelly continues, "I could see Pagans doing something like this."

"Pagans?" Poppa asks.

"Or, uh, bike people. I just use them as an example.

What do you think of their capabilities of doing something like this?" Kelly asks.

"For money, usually they'll do anything and the other thing is, are they gonna be so gone—" Poppa starts to say, and then asks, "What happens if he resists?"

"Oh he's gonna resist," Kelly asserts.

"What are they gonna do?" Poppa asks. "Are they gonna kill him?"

"Felony murder doesn't go down well," Kelly says.

"That's a bad resolution, let's put it that way," Moore interjects.

"Yeah."

"That's a big guy, I saw him. You're bigger than me. I'm looking up at him like—" Poppa starts to say.

"Well, I mean, that has to be thought out," Moore says.

"So what do I tell Newbold then? Nobody wants to kidnap this guy?" Kelly asks.

"No," Moore answers. "Now here, see, here is the thing I go back to from day one on, on that. You're not gonna snatch him off the street. Your problems with that are just too potentially, too great. One, he gets in his car in the underground basement."

"I've kidnapped enough people that I know there's a problem and, and he, he, uh, is the worst of all," Kelly says.

"Well, what about that other plan we were talking about?" Poppa asks.

"All right, the girl," Moore says, referring to the temptress.

"Right."

"If he is interested in the girl, she can set up the biker and that then reduces an awful lot of problems. In other words, I guess what I'm saying is this. If I were going to recommend anything to Newbold, I would say two things. We need to do a background on the woman, on the wife," Moore explains.

"That goes without saying," Kelly says.

"You need to know, and you've put it off too long. And we need to know if there's any sign of friendship or what's the best thought process is going to be, should the shit hit the fan. We need to absolutely have that reading. That's protection for you, Newbold, that's protection for us. That's the first thing. The second thing is, based upon that information, the next thing we need to do here is would sex work? Would sex get him out of the earth? Can we do it sexually?" Moore says.

"I'm sure it would. I'm sure that it would," Kelly interjects.

Moore continues, "It has the advantage of having Lewis partake in his own kidnap. Because he's gonna cover his tracks, he's not gonna tell the LaRouchies where he's going. He can sneak out to his car and he's going, oh man, blonde pussy, he's down the road, okay. He drives up, he ends it there; the house can be set, the location can be controlled, it can even be a motel room and the No Tell Motel."

Kelly likes the idea. "If you have control, it can be a very romantic kidnapping. If you control things it's much better. I mean you walk into the room, and say, we are going," he says, rehearsing giving Lewis orders. "It's a lot better than getting people unexpectedly off the street."

"And if he's in a strange area. He's in the No Tell Motel, you know. The managers don't want any problems, just because the customers are smiling and grinning and he's gone. His car ends up parked at the airport in Philadelphia. And we're off to a party," Moore concludes his scenario.

"And to the authorities, it becomes very cloudy," Kelly says. "Well, he went with this girl, and the cloudier it gets, then the whole sex debate comes up."

"Mm-hmm," Moore agrees.

"Assuming you get him, and you're talking to him, and he just says fuck you, I'm not buying any closer. What do you do now? How is everything going to be protected if it's just not cutting it with him?" Poppa asks.

"With him, I'm worried, and maybe I'm worried for valid reasons and maybe I'm not, but I'm worried, if we get to that point," Kelly says. "The only possible way you can bail out on this would be if we could convince him— because if he's not buying this thing, he's very much into the LaRouche mentality, and like with this girl I did the wrong number on her, and she's confused as to what it's all about, and he thought this was some kind of CIA plot, she thinks, so that he doesn't really know what it was about. And should he ever report it to anybody, it's too confusing, too bizarre, much like the *National Enquirer*. There's a potential, with him unafraid, that we could get him some wonderful place, spend the money for it, and then not get anything. It's possible. And he may not buy the safety device," Kelly answers.

"Would he be, being the LaRouche organization, do you think he would go to the cops? Being as how they hate the cops to begin with, anyway. I mean, obviously their view of the Bureau and everybody else is, they're all against them. What do you think the option is, there we'll be left with?" Poppa asks.

"They like—they like newspaper publicity. They like lawsuits. They like the challenge. It gives them—the worst thing for the LaRouche organization is to ignore them. He has, they'd be back in the media and they've got the name and it's sexy, and this would be good to keep them going for a long period of time," Kelly answers.

"Well, yeah, but the other thing to do is to make a death threat so that he's convinced," Moore says.

"To LaRouche?" Kelly asks.

"No. To Lewis." Moore says.

"To Lewis?" Kelly asks.

"Rich buys you a lot of things, but it doesn't buy you life," Moore says, in a mock philosophical tone.

"What do you mean? The cops will kill you?" Poppa asks.

"Mmm-hmm," Moore affirms.

"This is getting very bizarre. I think the whole thing is a very shaky deal," Kelly interjects. "What's your feeling?" he asks, turning to Poppa.

"I've never done it. I don't know other than what Don says. It was my impression that was what, if we get him, and he, you know, says, I'm sick of hearing and I don't buy anything you're saying and now, I'm gonna get a laugh because I'm gonna come back and I'm gonna get you," Poppa says.

"A real problem. And he might be inclined to do that," Kelly responds.

"That's the one fear that I have with the biker routine or the mercenary routine, is that something could go wrong and you could wind up with a—" Kelly says.

"Those guys pointing the finger at you?" Moore asks.

"No," Kelly says.

"Oh, all right. You mean sneakers up in a ditch," Moore says.

"Yeah. Which my conscience would have a problem

with, but also scares me. I don't get scared of too many
things, but that scares me. Because I can talk my way
out of almost any grand jury regarding abduction, but I
don't think I can talk my way out of a grand jury—" Kelly
says.

"Regarding a murder rap or—" Moore completes the
sentence.

"And the conspiracy would go right up," Kelly finishes.

◆ ◆ ◆

Using the excuse that he's going to start serving Cynthia
Kisser's lawsuit papers, Poppa then leaves Moore's house.
He has been told by the FBI they plan to arrest Moore
and Kelly at 4:00 p.m.

Once out the door, he puts one final message on his
tape recorder: "1425 hours. I never heard so much bull-
shit in all my life. Unbelievable. Unbelievable. Yeah, a
felony murder's going to be on my conscience. Sick bastard. AMF. Turning off the machine."

16 | You Don't Have Any Overt Acts

A little over an hour after Doug Poppa leaves Don Moore's house on September 30, FBI agents knock on the door. The agents, dressed in raid jackets with the letters "FBI" emblazoned across the back, inform Moore and Galen Kelly that they are under arrest, charged with conspiracy to kidnap Lewis du Pont Smith and Andrea Diano Smith. The two men are stunned. Just one week ago, at lawyer Bob Point's office, Moore had assured Kelly and Point, "We'll have zero problem in Loudoun County."

One of the agents tells Moore he has been secretly tape-recorded for the last three months by Doug Poppa.

"You don't have any overt acts," Moore blusters.

The agents take Moore and Kelly in handcuffs to waiting cruisers. They are driven to the Alexandria, Virginia Detention Center, where they will spend the night pending a bail hearing in the morning.

While Moore and Kelly are being taken to jail, FBI agents execute a search warrant at Moore's house. The agents seize financial documents, surveillance photographs, and other documents related to the Cult Awareness Network.

At the same time this is going on, E. Newbold Smith up in Pennsylvania has been informed that he is named in the same criminal complaint. His attorney arranges for him to surrender to authorities the next morning at the U.S. District Court in Philadelphia. FBI agents from the Newtown Square office execute a search warrant on Newbold's house.

"Biker Bob" Point, also named in the complaint, is arrested in New Jersey. FBI agents in New York execute a search warrant at Galen Kelly's house in Esopus, seizing financial records and other documents.

Doug Poppa, at the request of the FBI, is moved to an undisclosed location for his protection.

News of the arrests spreads rapidly. Some news media were tipped off in advance, and photographers catch Moore and Kelly being brought out in handcuffs. Washington TV stations carry the story on the evening news. Doug Poppa is interviewed on Washington's CBS affiliate, WUSA, describing the kidnapping plot. Reporters gather around Newbold's mansion in Radnor, Pennsylvania, but Newbold refuses to comment.

◆ ◆ ◆

The next morning, Moore and Kelly are brought before a U.S. magistrate in Alexandria. The ADL scrambles to protect its assets, sending Mira Lansky Boland, one of Moore's controllers, and Mark Rasch down to the courthouse to represent Moore. Rasch is a former Justice Department lawyer who assisted the unsuccessful prosecution of LaRouche in Boston, and the Alexandria railroad-trial. He has longstanding ties to the ADL, and is now working for the ADL's Washington, D.C. law firm, Arent, Fox, Kintner, Plotkin and Kahn. He and Moore became friends when Moore, as a special Deputy U.S. Marshal assigned to the LaRouche prosecution, slept on his couch in Boston in 1988. Now, Rasch conceals his former relationship with Moore. He tells the news media he is only a friend of Moore's family.

The magistrate releases Moore on a $250,000 bond and requires him to wear an electronic monitoring device that monitors his whereabouts.

Assistant U.S. Attorney Larry Leiser requests Kelly be denied bond. Leiser says Kelly is a flight risk, citing the D.C. and New York kidnappings as evidence that he is a danger to the community. The magistrate orders Kelly held in jail, and schedules a preliminary hearing for October 6, ironically the sixth anniversary of the infamous Leesburg raid against LaRouche associates' offices there.

Newbold Smith appears before U.S. Magistrate Richard A. Powers II in Philadelphia. He is released on his own recognizance after signing a $250,000 bond. Point is released on $10,000 bond by a New Jersey magistrate. All four men are ordered to appear before U.S. Magistrate W. Curtis Sewell in Alexandria on October 6.

◆ ◆ ◆

Cynthia Kisser and other CAN spokesmen immediately take to the airwaves. The government's complaint names the Cult Awareness Network, so Kisser is reluctantly forced to admit that Kelly, Moore and Newbold are associated with CAN. "We're not a criminal organization, we don't engage in kidnappings," Kisser protests. She claims that even though CAN advocates deprogramming, it does not endorse kidnapping.

The government has seized Kelly's financial statements which list thousands of dollars of payments from CAN during the time he was planning the kidnapping of Lewis du Pont Smith and Andrea Diano Smith. E. Newbold Smith is a funder of CAN. FBI wiretaps on Moore's phone have captured Kisser's conversations with Moore.

For the next week, disparate elements of the LaRouche prosecution team organize to defend the kidnapping conspirators. They fear that a conviction of such a central prosecution operative as Moore could unravel the LaRouche prosecution. The prosecution of this federal crime is becoming eclipsed by the spectacle of LaRouche's enemies scrambling to protect their own illegal activities.

At the October 6 hearing, the gaggle of LaRouche's enemies is out in force. Mira Lansky Boland again accompanies Moore. And E. Newbold Smith's attorney is former LaRouche prosecutor John Markham.

◆ ◆ ◆

John Markham had been the lead prosecutor in the 1988 federal LaRouche case in Boston, and co-prosecutor in the LaRouche trial later that year in Alexandria. Markham had used Moore as one of his chief investigators on the Boston LaRouche case, for which Moore served as a special Deputy U.S. Marshal. Now, Markham was defending not only Moore, Newbold Smith and Galen Kelly; he was also trying to save the LaRouche prosecutions.

Markham also had close ties to CAN. He had been scheduled to be the featured dinner speaker at CAN's 1990 national conference in Chicago. Galen Kelly was in charge of security for that conference.

But Markham, the "devil's advocate," had an even

more nefarious past. He was the official legal representative of the Process Church of the Final Judgement, an avowedly Satanic cult which openly promoted the use of drugs and deviant sexual behavior. Author Maury Terry, in his book *The Ultimate Evil,* presents evidence linking the Process Church to the infamous Son of Sam serial murders in New York City in 1976 and the California-based Charles Manson murder cult.

This was also not the first time attorney Markham had represented Newbold Smith. They had met while Markham was still working on the LaRouche case. Markham would later admit that Smith had told him at that time that he wanted to kidnap his son, Lewis. Markham, as a federal prosecutor, had told Newbold that kidnapping was illegal.

So Markham was no stranger to Newbold Smith's plans to lure Lewis Smith into the hands of Galen Kelly. In 1990, Markham, by now in private law practice, had approached LaRouche's attorney, Odin Anderson, and leading LaRouche associate Warren Hamerman, with a request from Newbold Smith. Markham told Hamerman and Anderson that Smith was willing to use his influence with President George Bush to help free LaRouche from prison, if they would arrange for Lewis Smith to work on an anti-drug program with Galen Kelly. The only conditions were that Lewis would have to move to Newburgh, New York, leave his wife, Andrea, and work under Kelly.

When the proposal was presented to Lewis Smith, he flatly refused.

◆ ◆ ◆

One hour before the scheduled start of the preliminary hearing on October 6, 1992, the grand jury hands down an indictment of Moore, Kelly, Smith and Point. All four are charged with conspiracy to kidnap. Moore is charged with soliciting Doug Poppa to commit a felony.

At 3:00 p.m., Kelly, dressed in the green and khaki overalls of the Alexandria jail, is brought before Magistrate Curtis Sewell for a bail hearing. Assistant U.S. Attorney Larry Leiser argues that Kelly is a flight risk and a danger to the community. He releases a partial transcript of the recording Poppa made at the meeting in Point's office on September 16. Leiser again cites Kelly's involvement in the D.C. kidnappings as evidence that he's dangerous.

Kelly's lawyer, Harvey Perritt, asks for bond. He offers a stack of letters written on Kelly's behalf as evidence that he is an upstanding member of the community. The letters are written by Kelly's fellow deprogrammers and CAN officials, including Jewish Defense League member Rabbi Tsvi Kilstein, a participant in the September 1991 New York kidnapping and deprogramming Kelly had carried out, and Herb Rosedale.

Rosedale is a partner in the New York law firm of Parker, Flatau, Chapin & Klimpl, and a board member of the American Family Foundation. Rosedale's law firm is the primary representative in the United States of Bank Leumi and Bank Hapoalim, two of the largest Israeli banks, which banks have been linked to drug money laundering.

Judge Sewell pays little attention to the letters, but grants Kelly bail anyway, saying that Moore is as central a figure in the conspiracy as Kelly, and that if Moore is let out on bail, Kelly should be also. He orders Kelly to sign a $250,000 bond, and to submit to electronic monitoring. An arraignment hearing is set for October 14.

Then, a week after Kelly's bond hearing, the grand jury hands down a superseding indictment. In the new indictment, ex-New York cop Tony Russo is charged for his involvement in the kidnap plot, prior to Poppa's turning on his tape recorder. Newbold is added to the solicitation count.

At 9:00 a.m. on October 14, all five defendants appear before chief U.S. District Judge James Cacheris, in the same courtroom where, almost four years earlier, Lyndon LaRouche had appeared as a defendant on trumped-up fraud charges. All five kidnapping conspiracy defendants plead not guilty. A trial date is set for December 14.

In 1984, Judge Cacheris had presided over a libel action brought by Lyndon LaRouche against the ADL and the NBC-TV network. Cacheris's rulings in that case were so biased against LaRouche, that the judge had avoided sitting on any case involving LaRouche since then. The kidnappers' case is soon transferred to Judge Timothy Ellis.

17 | I'll Blow the LaRouche Investigation Sky High

As both sides in the case *U.S. v. Smith, et al.* file pre-trial motions, portions of the transcripts of Doug Poppa's tape recordings are released, indicating that a scandal bigger than Watergate is unfolding. Poppa has not only captured evidence of the kidnapping conspiracy, he has captured evidence that could potentially overturn LaRouche's 1988 conviction.

Don Moore himself had already threatened this possibility. After the May kidnapping, Moore went on a public campaign against Loudoun County, Virginia Sheriff John Isom, beginning with a May 21, 1992 letter to the editor printed in the *Loudoun Times-Mirror*, in which Moore wrote:

"When the planning was conducted for the October 1986 search warrant 'raid,' using 475 men and women from the state police, FBI, ATF, IRS, Secret Service and, at my insistence, the Sheriff's office, Isom never attended the meetings. Instead, he was off hunting in Mississippi with 'General-for-Life' Herb Bryant.

"When Attorney General Mary Sue Terry asked Isom

136

to second her nomination for her current term as attorney general, he was so ignorant of the LaRouche case that he ordered me to write his speech and then read it just like I wrote it. (The *Times-Mirror* liked it so much they published it a week later.) . . .

"I could go on for days but I will close by stating that, if John R. Isom wants to debate this issue under any format at any time, I will be overjoyed to do so. Just tell Frank Raflo to bring some extra food—because I plan to eat Isom's lunch in public."

Before launching his campaign, Moore also called up Virginia Assistant Attorney General John Russell, the chief prosecutor for state AG Mary Sue Terry on the Virginia LaRouche cases. Moore warned Russell that if Democrat Mary Sue Terry took action to defend fellow Democrat John Isom, Moore would "blow the LaRouche investigation sky high."

On July 17, 1992, Moore told Ann Curley, a Loudoun County Democratic activist who had turned against Isom, about his conversation with Russell. In that conversation, captured by the FBI wiretap on Moore's phone, Moore says he told Russell, "I want you to understand one thing. I'm about to take a head shot at John R. Isom over the LaRouche matter. If Mary Sue, and this is my exact quote, 'If she rides into town to rescue John R. Isom, I will blow her out of the saddle and I will eat her horse.' And Russell said, 'I hear you.'"

Russell, Markham, and Mary Sue Terry all had a lot to fear from Moore. The LaRouche cases were riddled with massive government misconduct. As Moore himself said, "It was one black bag job after another."

◆ ◆ ◆

The formation of the "Get LaRouche" strike force, of which Moore was a principal member, began after former Secretary of State Henry A. Kissinger wrote a letter to then-FBI Director William Webster in 1982, asking Webster to take action against LaRouche. Subsequently, the President's Foreign Intelligence Advisory Board ratified Kissinger's proposal, asking Webster to investigate the finances of the LaRouche movement.

Kissinger and his cronies had hated LaRouche for years. In 1983 that hatred erupted into an all-out effort to kill or jail LaRouche.

Two developments in particular had sparked Kissinger's reaction. In 1982, LaRouche, after meeting with then-Mexican President José López Portillo, drafted a proposal for world monetary reform called "Operation Juárez," released just weeks before Kissinger's letter to Webster. The proposal called for a moratorium on Third World debt, and for extending new credit to the developing countries for industrial and agricultural development projects. "Operation Juárez" was a direct attack on the plans of the international banks to use the high level of indebtedness of these countries to impose Nazi-like economic looting policies on these countries. LaRouche argued for economic development to support a growing population. The bankers wanted to reduce population, and they didn't care if that was accomplished through underdevelopment, as well as famine and disease.

LaRouche's plan was not merely an academic proposal. In September 1982, the Mexican President took a first step in that direction, when he nationalized the banks. Kissinger reacted, bringing massive pressure on the Reagan administration to crush "Operation Juárez," and its author, Lyndon LaRouche.

In March 1983, LaRouche delivered another blow to geopolitician Henry Kissinger when President Reagan adopted LaRouche's proposal for the Strategic Defense Initiative. The plan called for advanced-technology weapons that could shoot down nuclear missiles in flight. The SDI, if put in place, would destroy the "condominium" Kissinger had carefully worked out with the Communist leaders of the Soviet Union to dominate the world through the reign of nuclear terror, known as Mutually Assured Destruction. Kissinger's buddies in Moscow joined in attacking LaRouche, making LaRouche public enemy number one in the Soviet press.

In 1984, LaRouche ran for President, campaigning vigorously on these achievements and exposing his enemies. By the end of the campaign, the "Get LaRouche" strike force had swung into high gear.

◆ ◆ ◆

A grand jury was convened in Boston by then-U.S. Attorney William Weld, a Boston Brahmin patrician from the same social class as E. Newbold Smith. For nearly two years, Weld was unable to bring any criminal charges.

After two LaRouche associates, Janice Hart and Mark Fairchild, won statewide Democratic primaries in Illinois in March 1986, the "Get LaRouche" strike force redoubled its efforts. A general assault in the media was launched to vilify LaRouche. A coalition was formed among Weld, Virginia Attorney General Mary Sue Terry, New York Attorney General Robert Abrams, California Attorney General John Van de Camp, and others with the intent to bring trumped-up charges against LaRouche associates, in as many jurisdictions as possible. Don Moore was an asset of every one of these agencies.

In the summer and late fall of 1986, the Soviet press stepped up its attacks on LaRouche, calling on U.S. officials to prosecute him. Prior to the U.S.-Soviet summit meeting in Reykjavik, Iceland, the Soviets demanded LaRouche be imprisoned by the United States government as proof of the government's good faith, for a summit to take place with Gorbachov.

In October 1986, acceding to Soviet pressure, Weld handed down his initial indictments, following the infamous Leesburg raid.

Then, in February 1987, Mary Sue Terry, relying on Don Moore, indicted 16 individuals and five corporations in Virginia. One month later, in March 1987, state Attorney General Robert Abrams indicted 16 persons in New York. In the New York cases, charges were later dismissed against all but four persons. In their trial, one was acquitted, two each were acquitted on one of two counts, and one was convicted on all counts.

When the massive raid and criminal indictments failed to collapse the LaRouche movement, the U.S. Attorney in Alexandria, Henry Hudson, using an affidavit supplied by Don Moore, brought an unprecedented involuntary bankruptcy action in April 1987 against three publishing companies associated with LaRouche. This action was subsequently ruled illegal by federal bankruptcy Judge Martin V.B. Bostetter in the Eastern District of Virginia.

In May 1988, Weld's Boston prosecution of LaRouche and six associates, two corporations, two campaign committees and one association ended in a mistrial because of government stonewalling. The jury foreman announced publicly, and it was printed in the *Boston Herald,* that the jury would have voted to acquit on all counts. The judge, Robert Keeton, said the government was guilty of "institutional and systemic prosecutorial misconduct."

But the disintegration of the Boston prosecution didn't stop LaRouche's enemies' drive to put him in jail. Five months later, Alexandria U.S. Attorney Henry Hudson indicted LaRouche and seven others. Within 34 days, LaRouche was brought to trial, in the Eastern District of Virginia's infamous "rocket docket." Chief Judge Albert V. Bryan, Jr. presided. Bryan is tied to freemasonic circles, and through his connection as attorney of record to the Interarms company, was tied to the CIA's international arms traffic.

Judge Bryan's conduct in the LaRouche trial generated international outrage. He denied LaRouche a fair and impartial jury. He denied LaRouche the right to present a full defense. He allowed the government to present a lying version of the case. And in the end, he showed his bias completely by sentencing LaRouche, who was then 67 years old, to a virtual life sentence of 15 years.

Now, in that same Alexandria courthouse, LaRouche's former prosecutors are defending their own criminality.

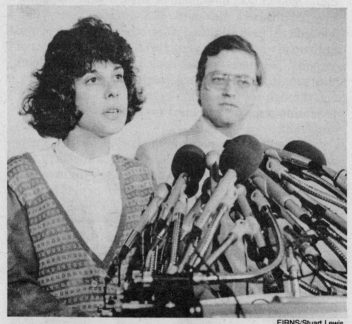

Illinois candidate for Secretary of State Janice Hart, and Lt. Governor candidate Mark Fairchild, after they won the Illinois Democratic primary in March 1986. That victory sparked the Get LaRouche strike force's move to bring trumped-up criminal charges against LaRouche and his associates, seeking to stop LaRouche's political movement.

EIRNS/Stuart Lewis

▲ LaRouche associate Rochelle Ascher, currently serving a ten-year sentence in a Virginia prison, for "securities violations."

◄ Lyndon LaRouche, now age 70, has served four years of a 15-year prison sentence—an effective life sentence.

▼ Michael Billington, a LaRouche associate serving a barbaric 77-year sentence in a Virginia prison, for violating Virginia's securities laws.

EIRNS/Stuart Lewis

EIRNS/Stuart Lewis

CHAPTER TWO

The Unmasking of Michael Rokos

In October 1990, CAN president Michael Rokos resigned from his position, amid a flurry of publicity that exposed his previously hidden criminal record.

Rokos had served on CAN's national board of directors for four years and had been an active member of the Baltimore CAN affiliate before his election as CAN's national president in October 1989. As president, Rokos had been active as a national spokesman for CAN, attacking many religious groups with vicious and hate-filled statements.

As documents revealed and as many news media reported in October 1990, Rokos had been arrested in Baltimore in July 1982 and found guilty on the charge of "soliciting lewdness".

Details of Rokos' arrest and sentencing were documented in an eight-page affidavit by the former Baltimore police vice squad officer who was posing as a minor when he arrested Rokos and in Baltimore Police Department records regarding the incident.

Hidden Criminal Past

Rokos' past had remained effectively masked under a carefully cultivated public image as local church vicar and chaplain for the Maryland State Police.

According to the affidavit of the undercover officer who arrested Rokos, Rokos violated a Maryland statute under which it is illegal to "procure or to solicit or to offer to procure or solicit for the purpose of prostitution [or] lewdness. . . ."

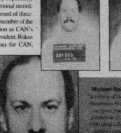

Michael Rokos, president of the Cult Awareness Network, was fired from his position in October 1990 amid a flurry of publicity charges revealing that he had been found guilty on the charge of "soliciting lewdness."

According to Article 27, Section 16, of the Maryland Penal Code, "the term 'lewdness' shall be construed to mean any unnatural sexual practice."

The undercover officer stated in his affidavit that he recalled the incident clearly because it was his first arrest as a vice officer. He had been assigned to the duty because he could still pass as a teenager. The officer could not forget what Rokos said to him.

This anti-CAN pamphlet features former Cult Awareness (CAN) president Rev. Michael Rokos, who resigned in October 1990, when it was revealed that he had solicited perverted sex from a male Baltimore police officer. Current CAN president Cynthia Kisser works closely with Kidnappers, Inc.'s Galen Kelly, Don Moore, and E. Newbold Smith.

Rokos' Shocking Request And Subsequent Arrest

According to the officer's affidavit, he was walking on the street when Rokos approached him, driving a white Volkswagen. When the officer refused an invitation to "go with him for a ride" to his "place in Bel Air," Rokos came out directly with what he wanted, asking the officer to commit a perverted and sadistic sexual act on him.

According to the officer's statement, Rokos said, "I want you to tie me up, put clothes pins on my nipples and make me suck your d - - k."

Following this startling proposition, the police officer gave a prearranged signal to his back-up officers that he was making an arrest and another officer came running toward the car. As the arresting officer related in his affidavit, Rokos promptly reached for the gear selector on the car, prepared to make a getaway.

"I immediately told him I was a police officer and, at the same time, thrust my right arm into the car and reached for the ignition key," the affidavit stated.

It continued, "The suspect immediately grabbed my right arm and forcibly pulled it towards his chest. This pinned me against the door jamb. Somehow I was able to turn the engine off during this time. I repeatedly yelled that I was a police officer and that he was under arrest. However, the suspect continued to resist my arrest . . . ."

"Although the arrest took place over eight years ago, I still vividly recall the incident. I recall the incident...

paper, for example, headlined its article on the unmasking of Rokos, "Cult Awareness Network Chief Charged as Pervert."

Despite the evidence regarding the incident, Rokos denied the charges. In an article in the *Baltimore Evening Sun* on October 25, 1990, under the headline "President of Cult Awareness Resigns," Rokos was quoted as saying, "The material they're spreading about me is an ... sentence."

... ever, that Baltimore Police ... akably showed that Rokos ... or solicitation and had ...

... e Baltimore Police Depart- ... een obtained which fully ... the arresting police officer.

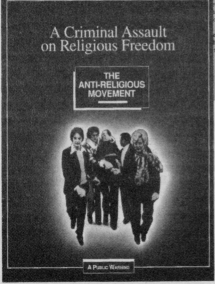

can cult awareness network n e w s

Alerting the World to the Dangers of Destructive Cults.

National Office: 2421 West Pratt Blvd., Suite 1173, Chicago, Illinois 60645

Volume VI, No. 10

October, 1990

CAN conference preview
Cult leaders and criminals-prosecuting the true perpetrators

Successful prosecution of cult members for criminal activity is not new. But often those prosecuted are not the ones ultimately responsible for the crime; it is the cult leader who conceived the crime, used undue influence on his or her followers to have them engage in criminal activity, and who benefited most from the criminal activity.

It is this uneven execution of the law, contradiction of the true spirit of the American legal system, that will be examined by attorney John J. E. Markham, II, speaker Saturday, Nov. 3 at the 1990 CAN National Conference. Markham participated in the successful government prosecution of Lyndon LaRouche and six of his followers on a federal court indictment alleging a 30 million dollar loan fraud.

Markham served in the U.S. Depart-

ment of Justice for six years, and was Special Assistant U. S. Attorney in Alexandria, Va., during the LaRouche trial. Markham's extensive trial experience includes having prosecuted cases for money laundering, fraud, loansharking, tax evasion, sex abuse and civil rights violations. He has participated in Grand Jury investigations and international extraditions.

Markham is currently Visiting Professor at the Santa Clara University Law School. He was an Advocacy Instructor for the Department of Justice Attorney General's Advocacy Institute for four years. He was Adjunct Professor at Harvard Law School for three years, and is the recipient of the Award for Distinguished Achievement in the Art and Science of Advocacy from the International College of Trial Lawyers. He is a graduate of Washington & Lee

John J.E. Markham, II

University School of Law.

Markham's presentation will focus on the various legal bases for prosecuting cult leaders for criminal acts they have initiated among their followers. He will highlight courses of action for making local prosecutors aware of how to develop cases with such a dimension as a viable legal strategy.

♦

Moon front group sues Moon organization

A renegade front group of the Unification Ch...

CAN's October 1990 newsletter featured an article promoting John Markham—former LaRouche prosecutor, and then attorney for E. Newbold Smith—as a speaker at CAN's 1990 national conference.

Other CAN operatives have included Virginia State Police investigator C.D. Bryant, who not only worked on federal and state LaRouche prosecutions, but also worked on behalf of CAN to dissuade LaRouche supporters like Helen Overington from continuing their support.

EIRNS/Philip Ulanowsky

John Overington and his mother, Helen Overington, on their way to a court hearing for LaRouche associate Rochelle Ascher. Mrs. Overington was "deprogrammed" by CAN and her children into renouncing her support for the LaRouche political movement.

EIRNS/Stuart Lewis

18 We're Not Going to Retry the LaRouche Case Here

The U.S. District Court for the Eastern District of Virginia, headquartered in Alexandria, is nicknamed the "rocket docket." Its procedures were carefully constructed over the years by Judge Albert V. Bryan, Sr., for whom the courthouse is named, and his son, Albert V. Bryan, Jr., who was chief judge until his recent retirement. The Bryan family has historically been powerful in Alexandria's banking and political establishment. They have been prominent members of Christ Episcopal Church, with close ties to Southern Freemasonry.

The "rocket docket" procedures, used to railroad LaRouche, are characterized by very rapid trial schedules, extreme hostility toward the constitutional rights of criminal defendants, and juries whose members are mostly federal government employees—especially law enforcement, the military, and the intelligence community—who are notoriously biased in favor of the government.

The trial of Kidnappers, Inc. would show that the "rocket docket" has another side.

142

♦ ♦ ♦

Between the time the Kidnappers, Inc. defendants are arrested on September 30 and their trial begins December 14, it looks like one section of the U.S. government is prosecuting another section of the U.S. government—the section to which the "Get LaRouche" strike force belongs.

John Markham, Newbold Smith's lawyer, relies on friendly elements in the news media to aid his cause—just as he had when he was an Assistant U.S. Attorney. Newbold's support group is joined by Patricia Lynch, formerly of NBC News and now at CBS. In 1984, while still at NBC, Lynch produced a libelous story for a prime time news magazine show, "First Camera."

That show featured the ADL's Fact-Finding Director Irwin Suall, New York Senator Daniel Patrick Moynihan (D) and other sources, many of them wearing disguises, retailing Soviet-inspired slanders against Lyndon LaRouche. Among Lynch's sources for that story were the ADL, former CIA counterintelligence chief James Jesus Angleton, and Priscilla Coates of CAN.

The NBC show's purpose was to force the Reagan administration to distance itself from LaRouche, as the Soviet government was demanding. The outlandish lies broadcast became the subject of LaRouche's 1984 libel suit against NBC. And John Markham had obtained his list of prosecution witnesses for the unsuccessful 1988 Boston prosecution from Lynch.

Now, Markham, speaking through LaRouche's enemies in the news media, especially the *Philadelphia Inquirer* and the Washington, D.C. TV stations, portrays the upcoming trial as the result of a tragic rift involving a father who desperately wants to extricate his son from what he considers to be a "criminal cult." A massive media effort is made to conceal the evidence that this "loving father" was so dominated by rage, that he would hire thugs like Galen Kelly and Don Moore to kidnap the son Newbold Smith supposedly loves.

◆ ◆ ◆

Government prosecutors counter Markham's maneuvering in a pre-trial motion. They ask Judge Ellis to prevent Markham from presenting evidence to the jury that the defendants were acting for a "good purpose," or were somehow justified in plotting to kidnap Lewis and Andrea Smith.

The government's court papers state, "Justification evidence would include evidence such as: 1) Lewis du Pont Smith was brainwashed; 2) he was incompetent; 3) he was tricked, fooled, programmed etc. into joining a cult or political organization; 4) he was squandering the family fortune (his share of which he legally and rightfully inherited); 5) he was ruining the family name, etc." The government argues that all these reasons are irrelevant, because under federal law, nothing could possibly justify kidnapping an adult.

The prosecutors go further, defending Lewis du Pont Smith's rights to have his political views and be free from the threat that he will be kidnapped by those who disagree with him. The same pre-trial prosecution motion says:

"The introduction of 'purpose evidence,' for example, that the LaRouche organization was a cult from which the defendants had to kidnap and 'deprogram' victims, will generate great press but will do little to advance the interests of justice. The defendants will call their cult experts to say the LaRouche organization was a cult; the government will call its experts to say it was nothing more than a political organization. They will call their people to say 'deprogramming' works; we will call ours to say that it is ridiculous to suggest that you can 'deprogram' someone out of their political positions. (We do not dispute that people can change their minds on particular positions when confronted with specific facts. However, that is not 'deprogramming'; that is called open dialogue and debate, and you do not have to kidnap someone as a prerequisite.) We can listen to testimony that Lewis du Pont Smith is incompetent and the defendants' 'purpose' was to save him as a result of that incompetence from an evil, corrupt political organization. The government can call its experts to show that Lewis du Pont Smith is not incompetent. (Having met with Lewis du Pont Smith and knowing his background, we are confident that the evidence would show that this University of Michigan graduate and former teacher at the Rectory School and the Friends Central School is fully competent.)"

Ironically, the government's motion here is 180 degrees different from what the government said about LaRouche and his political movement in 1988, when it was prosecuting him and his associates.

◆ ◆ ◆

A hearing is held on November 20, 1992 on the government's motions. The room is filled with journalists, CAN supporters and LaRouche haters, along with victims of CAN-linked kidnappings. The ADL's Mira Lansky Boland and CBS's Pat Lynch hover around the defense table, giving support to attorney John Markham and the conspirators. All the defendants except Newbold Smith are there; Markham says a "neurological" problem has prevented Newbold from appearing in person.

Prosecutor Leiser argues before Judge Ellis that he must not allow Markham to obscure the issues in the trial by attacking LaRouche, and thereby implying the kidnappers were justified in plotting their crime.

Markham, by now having had time to review the incriminating statements his client has made on tape, says he only wants to show there is another explanation for what the jury will hear on the tapes. He claims that Smith, Moore, Kelly, Point and Russo were not planning to kidnap Lewis and Andrea at all. The defendants were merely working with the ADL, CAN, private attorneys, and various law enforcement agencies to bring about the financial collapse of publishing companies associated with LaRouche, concocted criminal prosecutions of LaRouche supporters, and defamatory news articles about LaRouche—Moore's "busting the covey" scenario.

Markham further claims the tapes will show that Smith, Kelly, Moore and Point were only gathering information.

Leiser is incredulous. "Are you sure? You better go back and listen to those tapes again!" he says.

Four years earlier, Markham, as a government prosecutor, had denied that a politically motivated alliance existed among the government, CAN and the ADL and others that engaged in political dirty tricks and financial warfare against the LaRouche movement. In fact, the U.S. government has continued to rely on this argument to keep LaRouche in jail. Now, Markham's defense of his client, Newbold Smith, has become what, as a government prosecutor, he had previously denied.

Judge Ellis responds, "We're not going to retry the

LaRouche case here, Mr. Markham. I know that's what you'd like to do." Ellis rules there is no motivation that justifies a kidnapping. But Ellis also leaves the door open a crack for Markham. He rules that even though evidence that the LaRouche movement is a "cult" is irrelevant to the kidnapping charges, he will allow Markham to introduce such evidence to show his client's "state of mind" in bankrolling and planning a kidnapping.

At the end of the hearing, Leiser shocks the court-room by raising the possibility that Markham may be called as a witness. He gives Judge Ellis a copy of a letter Markham had written to Newbold when Markham was still a federal prosecutor. The letter refers to a conversa-tion Newbold had had with Markham, in which Newbold told Markham he was considering kidnapping his son, Lewis. Markham responded by advising Newbold that kidnapping is illegal. The letter is evidence that Newbold had considered kidnapping Lewis long before Doug Pop-pa's tape recorder was ever in the picture.

Judge Ellis is disturbed at the prospect of Newbold's lawyer being called as a witness. He orders Newbold to appear in court on November 25 to discuss the matter in person.

And a hearing is set for December 4, to decide what sections of the tapes will be played for the jury.

Judge Ellis issues a written decision on November 20, in which he rules that the defense will not be allowed to introduce "evidence concerning the nature of the Lyn-don LaRouche organization insofar as such evidence re-lates to establishing a motive for the alleged kidnapping. This court has ruled that motive is not a material element of a kidnapping offense." However, Judge Ellis continues, such "evidence may be used to refute the conspiracy charge or to provide an innocent explanation for conduct or statements relied on by the government to prove the elements of the conspiracy to kidnap charge."

Concerned that Markham will exploit Judge Ellis's ruling, prosecutor Larry Leiser files a motion for clarification, warning that Markham will try to get in through the back door, evidence that would not be allowed through the front door.

♦ ♦ ♦

On December 4, Judge Ellis holds a final hearing to determine which excerpts from the more than 60 hours of tapes will be played during the trial. Markham presses the judge to let him put on evidence that the LaRouche organization is a "criminal cult," from which the conspirators merely wanted to extricate Lewis.

Leiser counters; nothing justifies a kidnapping, he says. He stuns the courtroom when he says, "The LaRouche organization is not a cult."

Mira Lansky Boland and Pat Lynch audibly gasp. "According to Boland, the government prosecutor's portrayal of the LaRouche group as a political organization with little distinction from mainstream parties will give LaRouche fundraisers more ammunition to pry money from unwitting contributors," reports the *Philadelphia Inquirer*, in a wrap-up article printed December 27, as the trial was ending.

But Judge Ellis reiterates his previous ruling: Nothing justifies a kidnapping. He will instruct the jury to disregard any evidence that portrays the LaRouche organization as a cult.

At the end of the hearing, a list of prospective jurors is released. The list contains a statistically improbable number of people who live or work in Loudoun County, the home base of defendant Don Moore. The list includes the wife of a man who testified against LaRouche associate Rochelle Ascher at her 1989 trial in Loudoun County—a trial tainted by pre-trial publicity defaming the LaRouche movement.

Questions are raised as to whether the jury pool is being "stacked." Particular attention is focused on Henry Hudson, now the head of the U.S. Marshals Service, which plays a role in securing the jury pool. Hudson is the former U.S. Attorney in the Eastern District of Virginia, who had prosecuted LaRouche. Hudson has a lot to protect, since Moore was on his investigative team, and Markham had been his assistant in that prosecution. But Hudson was also linked with Moore's former boss, Loudoun County, Virginia Sheriff John Isom, with whom Hudson reportedly had gone hunting. More recently, in 1992, Hudson was reportedly under investigation for allegations the Marshals Service interfered with a D.C. police prosecution of ARGUS head J.C. Herbert Bryant, who had been arrested in Washington for carrying guns that were not registered in the District of Columbia.

♦ ♦ ♦

On the first day of the trial, December 14, the courtroom is packed. Before beginning jury selection, Judge Ellis again admonishes Markham. I don't think you understand my rulings, he tells Markham: "This is a case about conspiracy to kidnap and solicitation to kidnap. It is not a trial about the LaRouche organization or deprogramming people from a cult."

It takes the entire first day to select the jury, highly unusual for the Eastern District of Virginia's "rocket docket." By contrast, the jury in the LaRouche case in 1988 was selected in less than two hours. However, as it had been in the LaRouche case, this jury pool is also highly prejudiced against LaRouche. According to one observer, potential jurors range from hostile to extremely hostile to LaRouche. Jurors with a manifest bias toward LaRouche are seated.

"Kidnapping, let's call it what it is," assistant prosecutor John Martin tells the jury in his opening statement, quoting the words Don Moore spoke to Doug Poppa. Martin introduces the conspirators to the jury. Edgar Newbold Smith was the financier of the operation. He is the one who wanted the kidnapping to take place. He was upset because his son was a member of the LaRouche movement. Galen Kelly is a veteran deprogrammer. Don Moore considers himself an expert on the LaRouche movement. Robert Point is the lawyer who gave illegal advice. And Tony Russo is the operative who helped carry out the plans.

There was another figure in the operation, Martin tells the jury: Doug Poppa. But Poppa was working for the FBI, and wherever Poppa went, he took along his tape recorder. Poppa will give you a "ringside seat," Martin tells the jury.

Martin recounts how the kidnap plot developed. He tells the jury they will hear a lot of discussion on tape about the kidnapping plans. Most of the discussion was about three problems: how to kidnap Lewis, who was married, a big man, and not a willing victim. Second, how not to get caught. Third, where to take Lewis once he was kidnapped. The agreement to kidnap Lewis had already been reached before Poppa started his tape recorder; the discussion was only about how to do it. "They not only talked the talk, they walked the walk," Martin says.

At the close of the trial, Larry Leiser will speak to you again, Martin concludes, and he will ask you for a verdict: "Kidnapping, let's call it what it is."

◆ ◆ ◆

Lead defense attorney John Markham addresses the jury next. He admits that Newbold Smith talked about kidnapping his son. "I've got a hot flash for the government," Markham says, "E. Newbold Smith has been talking about kidnapping his son for years." Markham admits Newbold had hired Galen Kelly to deprogram his son; that he had hired Don Moore, because of Moore's involvement in the LaRouche prosecution. But, Markham says, it was all talk. Newbold was merely talking out loud about kidnapping Lewis—he never agreed to actually do it.

Galen Kelly's attorney, Harvey Perritt, speaks next. He, too, admits there was talk of kidnapping Lewis. He admits the jury will hear evidence that Kelly was involved in other kidnappings and is a deprogrammer. But he never agreed to kidnap Lewis because, being an expert kidnapper, he didn't think it would work.

Then Don Moore's lawyer, Stan Powell, addresses the jury. His job is to discredit his own client. He wants to convince the jury that everything Moore said on tape is an exaggeration or a lie. Everyone's here because of Don Moore's big mouth, he says. Moore is a bighearted man who helps anyone he can. He wanted to help a distraught father. He is a legend in his own mind.

"Biker Bob" Point's lawyer, Bernard Czech, tells the jury Point is simply a disabled cop who went to law school. Point has a medical problem, Czech tells the jury, he falls asleep a lot. You may see him falling asleep during this trial. He had nothing to do with the kidnapping.

When Tony Russo's lawyer finally gets his turn, he simply minimizes Russo's role.

◆ ◆ ◆

The government wastes no time in presenting its case. The first witness is Carol Hoffman, the New Jersey waitress and daughter of a cop who had been hired by Kelly and Moore to follow Lewis Smith, join his health club, and strike up a friendship with him. She testified to her numerous trips to Philadelphia with Kelly and Moore. She said she heard Kelly say they were planning to "snatch" Lewis.

After Hoffman, the government calls Doug Poppa to the stand. Painstakingly, the former police officer takes the jury through the kidnapping conspiracy, playing hours of his secretly made tape recordings. The jury listens intently as the foul-mouthed Moore, Kelly, Newbold Smith and Point talk of hiring motorcycle gangs or soldier of fortune-types to abduct Lewis and Andrea Smith. They hear Newbold say he wants his son "lifted" and brought to Kelly. They hear the conspirators talk about how they will avoid being caught.

For three days, the hours of tapes are narrated by Poppa, an expert police investigator who had at one time risked his life infiltrating drug gangs, and now risked his life infiltrating this conspiracy ring. After each segment is played, Leiser meticulously reviews the transcripts of the recordings the jury is hearing, asking Poppa to explain to the jury the intricacies of the plot and the peculiarities of the kidnappers' jargon.

The jury sits in rapt attention during the lengthy

testimony. Finally, they hear the tape recording made on September 30, when Moore and Kelly put the final touches on the kidnap plot. They hear Don Moore say that Lewis might end up dead: "sneakers up in a ditch."

And what did you do after you made this recording? Leiser asks Poppa.

I left the house at the request of the FBI.

And what happened next? Leiser continues.

They were arrested.

◆ ◆ ◆

Under cross-examination, Poppa cannot be shaken. As defense attorneys press him to put an innocent explanation on the conspirators' own words, Poppa emphasizes that what they were talking about is absolutely clear. Moore, Smith, Point, Kelly, and Russo were deadly serious about kidnapping Lewis and Andrea Smith; and they would have carried it out had they not been arrested.

Every attempt backfires. Moore's attorney Stan Powell tries to get Poppa to admit that Moore is an exaggerator whose words cannot be taken seriously. Kelly's attorney Harvey Perritt asks Poppa if anyone had told him about Galen Kelly besides Don Moore.

Yes, Poppa replies.

Who? Perritt asks.

The FBI, Poppa answers.

And what did they tell you? Perritt continues.

They told me that if Galen Kelly is involved with Moore it must be serious, because Kelly is under investigation for other kidnappings, Poppa responds.

The jury is shocked.

◆ ◆ ◆

All five defense attorneys try to impugn Poppa's credibility, implying that he is testifying for the government only because he is getting paid. When Poppa was first relocated from Virginia by the FBI after the conspirators were arrested, he was sent to a strange city. Having been fired from the Loudoun County Sheriff's Department, Poppa has not had a paying job for months. Because he was fired for being a whistleblower, the chances of his being hired by another police department are not good. A lawyer in the city where Poppa had relocated, had written the FBI demanding they pay Poppa $250,000 for his work as an undercover agent. The FBI refused, but finally agreed to pay him the equivalent of his Sheriff's Department salary, approximately $3,000 a month.

But Poppa stands his ground. He had been fired by Loudoun Sheriff John Isom because he helped get an innocent man out of prison, William Douglas Carter. He is testifying here because he had reported Moore's crime to the FBI. His life is now in a shambles. He is out of work, and he has had to move to a strange city for his own protection. "If I wanted to make money," Poppa says, "I would have kept my mouth shut."

After Poppa testifies, the government calls Loudoun Sheriff's Deputy Pete Becerra to corroborate Poppa's testimony about the initial approach by Moore, back in June. Becerra tells how he was present on June 26, 1992 when Moore first approached Poppa. He also testifies how, independent from Poppa, he also went to the FBI to report Moore's crime.

The government then has very little left to do to prove their case. They call several FBI agents to testify about the arrests and the searches.

◆ ◆ ◆

But Leiser also wants to call two of Kelly's other kidnap victims as witnesses. Fearing the impact this will have on the jury, all the defense lawyers agree to let Judge Ellis tell the jury about the kidnappings, rather than have the witnesses tell it themselves. Judge Ellis tells the jury, "It is hereby stipulated and agreed between the parties that if called in this case, witnesses would testify as follows: 1) Cara Schenker on September 17, 1991 was a 26-year-old woman and a 1988 graduate of Dickinson College with a degree in philosophy. At no time has she ever been a prostitute or have a boyfriend that was her pimp.

"On Tuesday, September 17, 1991, Cara Louise Schenker and her boyfriend were about to leave their apartment in New York, New York. At that time, she was abducted by several men she did not know. Two of these men were the defendant Galen Kelly and defendant Anthony Russo. Ms. Schenker resisted the men and was taken by them against her will. She was taken against her will by those men to a location in Pennsylvania where she was kept until Friday, September 20, 1991. And on that date, she was taken against her will to the home of defendant Anthony Russo. Ms. Schenker was kept at defendant Russo's home against her will.

"On the evening of Tuesday, September 24, 1991, defendant Galen Kelly took Ms. Schenker to Hazlet, New Jersey where she remained against her will until September 27, 1991, at which time she was returned to New York, New York. The day following her release, she reported her kidnapping to the Federal Bureau of Investigation.

"On May 4, 1992, Debra Dobkowski, age 36, was employed full-time at the Environmental Protection Agency. In addition, she had a part-time job as a security guard for Wells Fargo. She's a graduate of Oberlin College and Harvard University.

"On or about the evening of May 5, 1992, Galen Kelly and others forcibly kidnapped Debra Dobkowski against her will from a location in Washington, D.C. Ms. Dobkowski resisted, but was forcibly placed in a van and driven to a location in Virginia against her will. There the defendant Kelly and others made statements in Ms. Dobkowski's presence to the effect that they had taken the wrong individual. Following this, they returned Ms. Dobkowski to a location in Washington, D.C."

The government rests its case.

19 | Perjury!

It is now defense attorney John Markham's turn. His first witness is Phillip Parrish, the keeper of Newbold Smith's yacht, the would-be scene of Lewis Smith's deprogramming. Markham wants Parrish to establish that it would have been too dangerous to take the yacht into the Atlantic Ocean, say, 12 miles offshore, in late fall. But under cross-examination, Parrish admits the yacht could easily have sailed south to Belize, "where bribery is king," as "Biker Bob" Point had advised.

Markham's next witness is Chris Curtis, the former LaRouche associate whom Don Moore claimed he had "deprogrammed." Curtis, under threat of prosecution, had become a witness against LaRouche. In exchange, Markham and Moore helped Curtis get into George Mason University law school in Virginia.

Since joining the "Get LaRouche" strike force, Curtis has become friends with Moore. Curtis has also become fully integrated into the ADL and CAN brainwashing apparatus. As a prosecution witness, Curtis has lied before for Markham, and now, Markham is calling on his services again.

Curtis testifies he had been hired by Newbold Smith to find Lewis Smith in New Hampshire in 1988, when Lewis was living there, and running for Congress. According to Curtis's testimony, Newbold had discussed kidnapping Lewis with him. Curtis says he told Newbold that kidnapping wouldn't work. Markham gets Curtis to tell the jury he thinks the LaRouche organization is a cult, even though Judge Ellis has already ruled this should not be allowed.

Before adjourning for the weekend, Judge Ellis dismisses Tony Russo from the case, saying not enough evidence has been presented to link him to this conspiracy. On leaving the courthouse, a relieved Russo tells the media, "I can tell you the truth, I didn't have nothing to do with this."

♦ ♦ ♦

When the trial resumes on Monday, December 21, the defense makes a desperate attempt to discredit Doug Poppa's testimony.

Moore's attorney, Stan Powell, calls to the stand John Russell, a Virginia Senior Assistant Attorney General, and the prosecutor of the Virginia cases against LaRouche associates.

This is the same John Russell whom Moore called in May, threatening to blow up the LaRouche cases if Russell did not defend him. Now, John Russell, a sitting prosecutor, is testifying on behalf of Don Moore, one of his chief investigators in the state LaRouche cases. But Russell is not just interested in getting Moore off the hook for kidnapping; Russell is trying to cover for his own involvement in Moore's illegal intrigues.

"During the period of the last six and a half years, have you been able to observe the character and the demeanor of Donald Moore?" Powell asks.

"Yes sir, very closely," Russell responds.

"What was the character trait of Donald Moore when he was involved in these investigations with you, in terms of how he talked about the investigations, and how he conducted himself in the investigations?"

"Well, in my experience with Don Moore, he tended to talk in hyperbole, I guess is the best way to phrase it. He was prone to exaggeration, and also had a regular habit of using militaristic terms whenever he talked," Russell answers, referring to Moore's frequent "Vietnam" analogies.

"During the course of your association with Mr. Moore, how did he view the criminal investigations in which you were involved with him?" Powell asks.

"Again, as I said, he was prone to exaggerating them in both scope and consequence. It's something that I and the people in my position had to take into consideration."

"Did he tend to embellish what his role was in those investigations?"

"He did tend to place himself in a degree of greater importance than he actually served from time to time," Russell says. Then he takes aim at Poppa.

Powell asks, "Have you talked to people in the law enforcement community about Doug Poppa's reputation for truthfulness and honesty?"

"Yes, sir, in both—from police officers and prosecutors."

"Have you been able to develop an opinion about

what is the opinion of the law enforcement community for Doug Poppa's reputation for truthfulness and honesty?" Powell asks.

"I'm aware of his reputation, yes, sir."

"And what is his reputation?"

"His reputation is of an officer who would fabricate evidence to suit his purpose," Russell testifies.

But under cross-examination, Russell's fabrications begin to unravel. He admits he is a personal friend of John Markham, with whom he had gone to school. He admits that the only prosecutors who told him Poppa was unreliable were the prosecutors who opposed Poppa's whistle-blowing in the Carter case in Loudoun County, in which Carter had won a new trial, and an acquittal, based on Poppa's testimony. In that case the judge, in granting Carter a new trial, said Poppa told the truth and that the prosecutors had lied.

Russell is asked by prosecutor Larry Leiser to name the State Police officers on whom he is relying for his opinion of Poppa.

"I couldn't name all of them because it has been over a several year period of time," Russell answers.

"Just give us the ones you remember," Leiser asks.

"Almost all of them would have been state police officers assigned to the Fairfax Bureau of Criminal—Fairfax-based Bureau of Criminal Investigations."

"Just name five."

"The two supervisors in that office are the ones that I'm principally acquainted with—would have been Ralph Marshall and Warren Shand," Russell responds.

"And who else did you rely upon?" Leiser asks.

"I couldn't give you the names of the other officers because they weren't as well known to me—they were present during conversations. The two supervisors are better known to me, and those are the two names that I remember."

"But, Mr. Russell," Leiser persists, "you've come before this jury and indicated that a man is not to be believed, and you can only name two of the police officers when you indicated, or implied, at least, that there were numerous police officers?"

John Russell cannot answer the question. He claims he spoke with Marshall in October or November 1992, and that Marshall told him the State Police "could not rely on information furnished by Mr. Poppa as the basis for any affidavits for search warrants."

Then Russell is asked about his conversation with Warren Shand.

"And he, too, separately and apart, told you that you could not rely upon Mr. Poppa?" Leiser asks.

"He told me the same thing as far as what the State Police's position was on information which Mr. Poppa furnished," Russell answers. But Russell is lying. He hasn't spoken with Shand in years. And neither Shand nor Marshall has ever told him that Poppa was untrustworthy.

Later, on rebuttal, Warren Shand is called to the witness stand by the prosecution. Shand directly contradicts Russell. "Under your supervision, was Poppa ever the affiant of a search warrant?" prosecutor Larry Leiser asks.

"Yes," Shand answers.

"As his immediate supervisor at that time, would you have allowed him to be the affiant of a search warrant or an arrest warrant if you did not believe that he was truthful?" Leiser continues.

"No, I would not," Shand responds.

"Based on your own direct experience with Douglas Poppa, what is your personal view as to Doug Poppa's truthfulness?" Leiser asks.

"During the time that Mr. Poppa worked for me, he never, to my knowledge, lied to me. His affidavits for search warrants appeared to be good to me, and they were acted on properly by the courts," Shand replies.

"Do you know an attorney by the name of John Russell?" Leiser follows up.

"Yes, I do," answers Shand.

"At any time did you ever speak to Mr. Russell concerning the reputation for truthfulness and veracity regarding Douglas Poppa?" Leiser inquires.

"Not that I can ever recall," Shand responds.

"Special Agent Shand, if I were to tell you that Mr. Russell, from that very witness stand, said that he had spoken to you recently about Douglas Poppa's reputation for truth and veracity, what would your response be?" Leiser gets to the final point.

"He would be mistaken," Shand says, exposing Russell's testimony as a lie.

♦ ♦ ♦

Markham then calls Hank Smith, Lewis's younger brother. Hank claims that Lewis and Newbold had a close relationship before Lewis became associated with LaRouche. Hank says he travelled in 1986 to Leesburg, where Lewis was then living, to ask him to be best man at his wedding, and that Lewis refused to see him. Hank was not alone on that trip. He was accompanied by Galen Kelly.

On cross-examination, Hank admits that the relationship between Newbold and Lewis was not really so close. He concedes Newbold is prone to drunken rages and has physically assaulted his children.

◆ ◆ ◆

Nearing the end of the day, Judge Ellis commands, "Mr. Markham, call your next witness."

"I call Edgar Newbold Smith," Markham announces.

After Newbold takes the stand, Markham begins. "Describe your relationship with your son Lewis as he was growing up," Markham says.

"As my son Hank said, it was an extremely close relationship. We had a lot in common. He was physically more akin to my physique than perhaps the others, so therefore we related to one another in sports. And Lewis had an enormous—I suppose still has—an enormous heart. By that I mean, he was just a fine, fine person in every respect," Newbold says.

"Did you love him?"

"I certainly did."

"There came a time when your son Lewis began to associate with the LaRouche organization?"

"Yes."

"While your son was with the LaRouche organization, what were your personal emotional feelings towards him?"

"Well, I felt very sorry for him because it was clear to me that he had become a captive of a cult," Newbold says, skirting around Judge Ellis's ruling.

But any skirting around is not necessary. For the rest of the day, Judge Ellis allows Newbold to tell the jury hate-filled lies about Lewis and his relationship with LaRouche, exactly what Ellis himself had ruled was irrelevant. Prosecutor Leiser keeps objecting, then finally gives up.

Newbold claims Lewis "had been kidnapped mentally and physically into this organization." He claims he had no access to Lewis, and that Lewis had refused to talk to him because Lewis's "controllers" prevented any contact.

Newbold is lying. Lewis had been advised by his attorneys to cut off contact with his family, after Newbold filed the incompetency proceedings against Lewis. The attorney's advice was based on what happened with Newbold's repeated efforts to contact Lewis, to lie about what Lewis had said, and then use that lie against Lewis in the incompetency proceedings.

"Did you believe, based on your observations of what he had done, that he was brainwashed?" Markham asks.

"Yes," Newbold says.

But this is even too much for Judge Ellis. The judge interrupts the questioning to tell the jury, "As I've instructed you, ladies and gentlemen, the fact that the father may believe that the son was brainwashed is not an excuse or justification for a conspiracy to kidnap. However, you may consider the evidence that he believed his son was brainwashed, insofar as it may bear, if at all, on whether there are innocent purposes or reasons for doing other things involved in the overt acts, other than criminal purposes."

Newbold ignores Ellis's admonition. He testifies that he firmly believed Lewis was brainwashed and everyone else he talked to believed it, too.

He admits he asked Galen Kelly, Don Moore and Chris Curtis to surveill Lewis. "I wanted eventually to get him to Kelly or vice versa, for deprogramming."

"And by get him to Kelly, do you mean kidnap him?" Markham asks.

"I didn't—no, I didn't think in terms of kidnapping. But I allowed myself to drift off in the area of what would happen if we did this—if we simply lifted him. I used that phraseology, which is something I think I picked up from Don."

"Now, you'll recall a conversation that you had on tape that was taped between yourself and Don Moore on July 15th?" Markham asks.

"Yes."

"That's the conversation where you—one of the conversations where you were discussing kidnapping, correct?"

"Yes."

"Now, sir, why were you discussing kidnapping with Don Moore in July of 1992, if in the past people had told you it wasn't going to work, and you had said it wasn't going to work?" Markham asks.

"I just brought it up again just to see if another officer of the law—ex-officer of the law—had any new slants. And maybe I shouldn't have done it, but I did do it. I certainly never decided to go ahead on any of that, but I wanted to hear what Don Moore had to say."

Newbold admits he discussed kidnapping Lewis in 1986, 1987, 1988, 1990, and 1991. But each time, he says, he never agreed to carry it out. He claims the discussions were all hypothetical. He maintains he only wanted Moore to gather information which could be used to generate negative publicity for LaRouche and bring about civil and criminal legal problems for Lewis's friends. But he never agreed to kidnap Lewis and Andrea; he only discussed it.

♦ ♦ ♦

Before beginning cross-examination, Leiser approaches Judge Ellis at sidebar: "Your honor, Mr. Markham has brought out the issue of Lewis' inability or lack of family contact. Time and time again he asked him have you had any contact with Lewis, and he tried to create the impression that the LaRouche organization, or his being brainwashed, had somehow controlled Lewis to the extent that he has alienated his family.

"One of the reasons—the truthful reason for not having any association with not only his father, but his other family members, is because they brought the lawsuit against him which resulted in their having his estate put in a trust.

"Now, I would like to bring that out. I think fairness and justice would require that. We don't have to get into the competency, but the fact that he made such an issue out of that, it's only fair that the government be permitted to a limited degree to show that there was a very good reason—had nothing to do with LaRouche—as to why he did not want to have contact with his family."

Judge Ellis says he will allow Leiser to ask limited questions on this subject.

"Mr. Smith, in your direct examination you described to this jury a relationship of love and trust and great camaraderie between you and your son Lewis, correct?" Leiser begins his cross-examination.

"Correct."

"And that was mutual, was it not?"

"It was mutual."

"That no longer exists today, does it?"

"Correct."

"Do you feel that you have any part or role to play in that reality?"

"Can you be more specific?" Newbold counters.

"Yes. Do you believe, Mr. Smith, that the fact that your relationship with your son is not what you would like, or what it once was, has anything to do with some things that you have done over the past several years?" Leiser clarifies.

"That may be true, if you're looking at it through the eyes of somebody who has been brainwashed into believing just what you've said," Newbold bristles.

"Have you been brainwashed?" Leiser shoots back.

"Not that I know of."

"Well, I'm asking you. You have not been brainwashed. I'm asking, Mr. Edgar Newbold Smith, do you believe that you in any way have done anything that has contributed to the diminution of the relationship between you and your son Lewis?"

"In his mind the answer may be yes. In my mind, no."

"He didn't ask you that, Mr. Smith, he asked you whether you thought so," Judge Ellis interrupts.

"No," Newbold says flatly.

Soon, a disagreement flares, chiefly between Judge Ellis and Leiser. At another bench conference, the judge chastises the prosecutor. "Mr. Leiser, maybe I didn't make it clear. The lawsuit is not going to be in this—that lawsuit, the merits of it, what it decided, are not part of this case. Now, tell me succinctly what you're attempting to show."

"I'm attempting to show, as I told the Court earlier, to counter Mr. Markham's point that Lewis was irrational in his reasons for not contacting the family. That one of the reasons he had for not contacting his family was because his family took steps to deny him access to his estate. That's all I'm trying to show. I don't think I violated the spirit of our understanding earlier, Your Honor, at all," Leiser responds.

"Well, you did in this sense," Judge Ellis says. "I did not understand you previously to say that you were going to bring out that the legal proceedings had to do with his power over his estate."

"That was my purpose, Your Honor, and my only purpose. It wouldn't make sense—and that was the reason for which—"

Judge Ellis interrupts. "None of this is relevant. It doesn't matter why they brought the lawsuit. It doesn't matter. It doesn't go to whether or not there was an intent to kidnap."

"I've been the proponent of that from the beginning," Leiser counters. "But when Mr. Markham brings this out as a defense to this and he tries to—"

"That's not a defense," the judge repeats.

"It's not, but he brings it out nonetheless. It's totally not relevant. I've agreed from the beginning. But it has come out and—" Leiser protests.

"What has come out, Mr. Leiser?" Judge Ellis asks.

"The fact that Lewis is some kind of brainwashed kid who doesn't have—" Leiser responds.

"That's not relevant. I'm going to tell the jury that's not relevant," the judge says.

"I understand that, Your Honor, but it's before the jury. Mr. Markham has—" Leiser argues.

"They're going to follow my instructions, Mr. Leiser. They're going to follow the court's instructions," Judge Ellis says. He tells Leiser to move on. "You can argue anything you wish to argue, but this jury is going to be told, and I'll tell them in simple terms, it doesn't matter whether he thought he was or wasn't brainwashed. It doesn't matter whether he was hard to get to or wasn't hard to get to. None of that is an excuse or a justification for kidnapping or an attempt to kidnap. Let's proceed," he decides.

Leiser then takes up another subject. He asks Newbold about the time he broke into Lewis's house in Leesburg.

"You went to a locksmith, did you not, on that occasion?" Leiser asks.

"That's correct," Newbold replies.

"And you told him that you were the owner of your son's house."

"I told him I was Mr. Smith."

"But you led him to believe that you were the owner of your son's house."

"Well, if he believed that, I didn't change his mind."

"Did Lewis find out that you did that?"

"Yes."

"Do you think the fact that you did that may have something to do with the way he approaches you and the other members of your family?"

"No, I think the fact that his captors tell him to think the way he thinks has all to do with how he thinks about our family," Newbold sneers.

"Mr. Smith, do you think any normal father would break into his son's house when his son wasn't there?"

"I told you, Mr. Leiser, I didn't break into the house."

"No, you just went to the locksmith and tricked him into thinking you owned the house so he could get you into the house."

"I didn't trick him into thinking anything of the kind. I told you just exactly as it happened." This is not the first time Newbold has lied under oath about breaking into Lewis's house. In 1988, Newbold was asked to testify about the incident before Judge Wood, who had previously ruled Lewis incompetent. Newbold's lie was so blatant that Judge Wood advised him to leave the witness stand and consult a criminal attorney.

Now, Leiser asks Newbold if he accepted Lewis and Andrea's marriage.

"Yes, I accepted the marriage. I mean, with Mr. LaRouche as his best man and Mrs. LaRouche as her matron of honor is not my idea of free—operation of free matrimony, if you will. But anyway, they did become married. And as a parent, I didn't think it was appropriate to fight them," Newbold says.

"Mr. Smith—the fact of the matter is that when your son and his wife tried to get their marriage, if you will—I don't know if the word is correct—certified here in the United States, you opposed it, didn't you?" Leiser asks.

"Yes."

"You opposed that?"

"Because I thought it was phony in the beginning."

"Do you think the fact that you took legal steps not to have their marriage affirmed here, if you will, in the United States, might have had something to do with their attitude and approach and their access to you?"

"I can't deny that."

"So it isn't all the doings of the LaRouche organization?"

"What's not all the doings?" Newbold responds cagily.

"The fact that you don't have access to your son in part is at your own hand, is it not?" Leiser clarifies.

"I can't answer that," Newbold says.

◆ ◆ ◆

Leiser now turns to the tapes.

"On the first occasion that you met with Mr. Moore in June," Leiser asks, "did you ever discuss with him the kidnapping? And when I say kidnapping, Mr. Smith, whether you used the words lift or grab or snatch, can you and I agree that all of those terms are—"

"Yes," Newbold says.

"Did you ever discuss with Mr. Moore at the end of June, kidnapping your son Lewis?"

"I don't think I did, sir, but if the tapes say otherwise, I'll yield to the tapes. But I don't recall saying anything to him at that time."

"Clearly you hired Mr. Kelly to give you guidance and advice about deprogramming, correct?" Leiser asks.

"Yes."

"In each of those years, but one, from '86 through '92, despite the fact that Mr. Kelly told you discussing kidnapping with regard to deprogramming was counterproductive, you nonetheless, by your own testimony, in each of those years discussed kidnapping, correct?"

"Well, only in the sense that I would bring up the subject, say can't we just pick him up, something simple like that, which constitutes, as you say, an act of kidnapping. And would always do it as a question, not as a statement: Let's go do it. And the answer always came down that we shouldn't do it."

"But, Mr. Smith, if you knew it was counterproductive, why would you even bother discussing them if you knew it was going to do the exact opposite of what your goals and intentions were, which was to disassociate—"

"Your question is now compound," Judge Ellis breaks in, taking some of the heat off Newbold.

"You knew, did you not, sir, that there was no purpose in discussing something that would be counterproductive?"

"Yes, but I've made mistakes before. And I did continue to ask questions, which—I agree with you, in light of all that has happened—didn't make sense to ask, but I asked them. I was not really thinking in terms of kidnapping in the ordinary sense of the Lindbergh baby or something."

Leiser asks Newbold to look at the transcripts. "Turn to the next page, and you'll see Mr. Moore concludes to some extent, the conversation at the top of the page, by saying: 'Now so it gives—it gives Newbold plausible denial, gives me plausible denial, gives everybody plausible denial.' You wanted 'plausible denial,' did you not, Mr. Smith?"

"I never discussed it," Newbold claims.

"As the person that was paying Mr. Moore, isn't it true that you wanted him to create a scenario or a plan that would give you 'plausible denial'?"

"I certainly didn't go to Mr. Moore to create anything," Newbold answers defensively.

Leiser continues directing Newbold's attention to the discussion with Moore about surveilling Lewis's house.

"Now, when you talk about the surveillance part of the thing, you're not referring to determining who's going to move into your son's new house, are you?" Leiser asks.

"That's true."

"You're not?"

"I'm not."

"You're talking about the thing being the agreement that you had with Mr. Kelly and Mr. Moore and Mr. Point to have your son kidnapped?"

"That is absolutely not true," Newbold bristles. "It's the thing that Mr. Moore had talked to me about. Mr. Kelly is out of the picture—I never talked to him. Mr. Point I didn't even know at the time; In fact, I'd never heard of it."

"But you agree, too, that the thing refers to kidnapping?"

"It referred to a hypothetical type of operation that Moore discussed," Newbold evades.

"Can you find anywhere in the pages preceding that comment where somebody says this is just hypothetical or words to that effect?"

"No. But in previous conversations with Moore it was discussed in a hypothetical way."

"And the plan you're hypothetically talking about here clearly involves kidnapping?"

"Yes, I would agree with that."

"Mr. Smith, tell the ladies and the gentlemen of the jury why it is in this instance that if you believed, based upon what Mr. Kelly told you, kidnapping would be counterproductive, you would waste your time discussing kidnapping with Mr. Moore?"

Newbold continues to maintain everything was hypothetical. "The only person I had to talk with was Mr. Moore. I couldn't talk to Mr. Kelly, he wasn't around. And we talked about this thing hypothetically. And we had talked about it previously hypothetically. And he was talking to me as though Kelly were there, and it all required an approval from me. You know, this wasn't any final plan."

Leiser directs Newbold to another section of the transcripts. "And then you say, 'Okay, all right. Well, I must say, it really requires Galen. Maybe in a three-way conversation, maybe the three of us here—' Now, were you suggesting that it required a conversation to further discuss a hypothetical plan?"

"Absolutely."

"Even though you knew that Mr. Kelly had told you that hypothetical plan, the object of which was kidnapping, would be counterproductive?"

"Mr. Kelly wasn't even there."

Leiser presses on. "My question to you, Mr. Smith, is, are you telling us that you were proposing to get together with Mr. Kelly and Mr. Moore to discuss a hypothetical plan about kidnapping?"

"That's what I'm telling you."

Leiser directs Newbold to the place in the transcript where he and Moore are talking about whether their phones are safe from wiretaps.

"Now, when you said 'I think I'm safe here, I'm sure I'm safe here,' you were referring to your telephone, were you not?" Leiser asks.

"Safe from anybody who might be listening. I'm not going to talk about a hypothetical plan for kidnapping and have the world listening," Newbold answers.

"So you felt that even though your discussion was hypothetical, you needed to make sure that your phone was safe?"

"Absolutely. Especially from the LaRouche organization, which is what I was more concerned about. I didn't have the faintest clue that the federal government was listening to the conversation. I was much more concerned that the LaRouche organization would have been tapping Donny's lines," Newbold says.

"Do you know that wiretapping is illegal?"

"Yes—well, unless you have permission."

"Well, a court order, of course," Leiser clarifies.

"Yes. But it's widely done, I've been told."

"Do you think that the LaRouche organization could have gotten a court authorized wiretap on Mr. Moore's phone?"

"I doubt that."

"So you think they would have done it illegally?"

"If they had done it or if they were to do it I would presume they'd have to do it illegally. But I understand it's not a difficult thing," Newbold claims.

Leiser continues to confront Newbold with his own words and Newbold repeatedly retreats into the world of the hypothetical.

Finally, with Newbold still on the witness stand, Judge Ellis orders a recess. Court is adjourned until after the Christmas holidays.

◆ ◆ ◆

When the Court reconvenes on Monday, December 28, Newbold retakes the witness stand. Leiser wastes no time. He confronts Newbold with the September 30, 1992 tape on which Kelly is heard saying, "Newbold wants the ultimate solution." Moore says, "He wants the snatch"; and Kelly says, "Yeah."

"These men that were working for you, who were paid by you, knew what you wanted them to do, didn't they?" Leiser asks.

After a long pause Newbold repeats his litany: It was all hypothetical.

Newbold Smith's testimony is almost the entirety of the defense case. Kelly's only witness is his minister. Moore's only defense is a stipulation that he provided information to several law enforcement officials, most particularly Rick Munson of Minnesota Attorney General Hubert Humphrey's office. Point calls no witnesses.

20 The Fix Is In

On the evening of December 28, Judge Ellis makes a critical decision which portends the direction he wants the case of *U.S. v. Smith, et al.* to go.

After hearing hours of Newbold Smith's rantings that his son Lewis is a captive of a "criminal cult," prosecutor Larry Leiser wants to call Lewis Smith, his wife, Andrea, and Andrea's mother, Martha Diano, as rebuttal witnesses to show that Newbold Smith is a liar.

Lewis and Andrea are to testify that it was Newbold who had destroyed the relationship between father and son. They would tell how Newbold Smith had spent the last seven years in an obsessive effort to destroy their lives. They would tell the jury about his past attempts to kidnap Lewis, and his previous efforts to lure Lewis into the clutches of the expert kidnapper-deprogrammer-brainwasher, Galen Kelly.

Martha Diano is to testify about her own close relationship with her daughter and son-in-law, and about her own conversations with Newbold and Peggy Smith.

Newbold's defense attorney John Markham protests.

He has just succeeded in putting before the jury exactly what Judge Ellis had previously ruled was irrelevant: that the LaRouche political movement is a "cult." He does not want anything to disturb what has already happened.

Leiser argues hard. He confronts the judge with Markham's chicanery. He demands the right to show the jury the truth.

Ellis seems troubled by Leiser's arguments. Perhaps I let him go too far, Ellis consoles Leiser. But he won't budge. Lewis, Andrea and her mother will not be allowed to testify. Their testimony would be irrelevant, Ellis rules. Even though it is just common sense that the jury won't simply forget the hours of Newbold's rantings, the judge says he will instruct the jury in strong terms that they should disregard Newbold Smith's rantings about Lewis being brainwashed and the LaRouche organization being a criminal cult. There is no motive to justify a kidnapping, the jury will be told.

In a revealing comment, Judge Ellis tells Leiser, "Well, if I'm wrong, you can appeal."

"No, I can't," Leiser shoots back. An acquittal means the defendants walk out free men.

"You're right," Ellis corrects himself.

Without the testimony of Lewis, Andrea and Martha Diano, Leiser has a limited rebuttal case. He puts on Virginia State Police officer Warren Shand to show that John Russell lied. He calls the locksmith from Leesburg Lock and Key, who contradicts Newbold's testimony about breaking into Lewis's house. The locksmith testifies that Newbold gained entry into Lewis's house by claiming to be the owner. The locksmith says he reported Newbold's subterfuge to the police, because it was obvious to him Newbold had lied to gain entry into Lewis's house.

♦ ♦ ♦

Closing arguments take place on Tuesday, December 29. Leiser takes the jury back through Doug Poppa's testimony and the tape-recorded evidence. They have heard the conspiracy develop through the government listening post provided by Doug Poppa. Leiser dissects Newbold Smith's testimony, recounts the inconsistencies in John Russell's testimony, and points the jury to the evidence that Kelly has committed prior kidnappings.

"LaRouche is not on trial here," Leiser tells the jury. Looking the jury right in the eyes, with special emphasis on soon-to-be foreman Marc Bush, he reminds them that they had pledged to put aside any prejudice they might have against LaRouche and judge the case on the evidence. "I'm going to hold you to that," he says.

♦ ♦ ♦

In his closing, John Markham repeats, in many ways, that his client Newbold Smith only talked about kidnapping, but he never agreed to do it. He hired Galen Kelly to talk to Lewis. He hired Don Moore to follow Lewis. He hired Chris Curtis to gather information on Lewis. He told everyone he wanted Lewis out of the LaRouche movement. But he never agreed to kidnapping. Markham asks the jury to separate Newbold Smith from the others.

Harvey Perritt, Galen Kelly's lawyer, argues that Kelly was never serious about kidnapping Lewis. He knew how to do a kidnapping, and this was one kidnapping that wouldn't work. He never agreed.

Don Moore's lawyer, Stan Powell, attacks his own client. He calls Moore "the G. Gordon Liddy" of Loudoun County. No doubt they talked about kidnapping, but "Don Moore is full of crap." This was a "failure on the runway," he says of the kidnap plot.

Bernard Czech, Bob Point's lawyer, quotes an Elton John song about love of a father for a son. Peggy Smith breaks down crying, giving the news media their story for the evening news. Czech claims Point had little to do with the plot.

Larry Leiser gets the last word. He portrays Newbold Smith as a driven man willing to do anything to get Lewis away from LaRouche. If Newbold didn't want a kidnapping, why would he associate with Kelly, Moore and Point? There is a family tragedy here, Leiser tells the jury, but there is also the law. Edgar Newbold Smith is not above the law. Edgar Newbold Smith is not man enough to come here and say he made a mistake, that he might have gone too far. Instead, he claims the kidnap plans were all hypothetical. "He never met a hypothetical he didn't like," Leiser says.

Leiser asks the jury to listen to the tapes and return a guilty verdict.

◆ ◆ ◆

On the morning of December 30, Judge Ellis instructs the jury and sends them off to deliberate. Ellis's instructions explain the legal meaning of a conspiracy to the jury:

"The government must prove that the defendant under consideration and at least one other person knowingly and deliberately arrived at some type of agreement or understanding that they, and perhaps others, would kidnap Lewis du Pont Smith and/or Andrea Diano by means of some common plan or course of action as alleged," Ellis instructs. He explains, "It is not required to produce a written contract between the parties or even produce evidence of an express oral agreement spelling out all of the details of the understanding."

After instructing the jury further on the law, Ellis seeks to cure the effects of allowing Newbold Smith to rant about the LaRouche movement. He tells the jury such testimony is irrelevant: "It does not matter whether the LaRouche organization is a legitimate political organization or whether it is a cult. . . . The nature of the LaRouche organization is not an issue here. . . . Neither the LaRouche organization nor any of its members are on trial here," he states.

After Judge Ellis concludes his instructions, the jury begins deliberations.

At around 6:00 p.m., after listening to tapes all day, the jury sends out a question to the judge. The answer to the question is the beginning of the final nudge to get the jury to acquit.

The note, signed by jury foreman Marc Bush, reads, "As to Count II Solicitation. Did anybody have to ask Poppa to actually participate in a felony or ask him to perform an action which might aid in a felony? Is surveillance a felony if surveillance is used to further a kidnapping?"

The government wants the jury instructed that if Poppa was solicited to do surveillance for a kidnapping, then Moore and Newbold Smith are guilty of solicitation to kidnap. Prosecutor John Martin asks a rhetorical question: "Assume for a second that Poppa was not working for the government and that the kidnapping had gone through, and that all Poppa had done was to have done the surveillance. Would Poppa have been guilty of the substantive crime of kidnapping for having done that? Yes."

Ellis asks Markham to answer.

Markham argues that Poppa had to be solicited to do the actual kidnapping, not to merely aid the kidnapping by conducting surveillance.

Ellis knows the government is right on the law, but he apparently wants a different result. He asks Martin for any last words. Martin says, "I would respectfully ask the Court to tell the jury that, yes, the solicitation had to be for the crime of kidnapping but that under 18 USC 2, surveillance in furtherance of kidnapping would be a part of the kidnapping crime."

Judge Ellis's response indicates that he knows what he is about to do is wrong. "It is not an easy issue so I, to some extent, mistrust the clarity with which I think I see it," he muses out loud. Then, he gives the jury a misleading answer and even rephrases their question.

He tells the jury, "So the answer is: Did anybody have to ask Poppa to actually participate in a felony? Yes. And the felony is kidnapping and abduction. . . . The next part of the question is: Or ask him to perform an action which might aid in a felony? No."

Ellis continues, "The next question is: Is surveillance a felony if the surveillance is used to further a kidnapping?" Ellis knows the law says the answer is yes; but if he says "yes" to the jury, they will have to convict the defendants. So Ellis rephrases the jury's question. "I take it by that you mean is surveillance the felony under the statute? No . . . the indictment says the felony is the kidnapping and abduction. . . ."

This final answer has a doubly misleading effect,

because it confuses the jury on the law of conspiracy which is Count I. Under standard conspiracy law, surveillance in furtherance of a kidnapping is illegal.

After another hour of deliberations, the jury goes home for the night.

◆ ◆ ◆

At 10:24 a.m. the next morning, jury foreman Marc Bush sends out another note which reads: "If the defendants agreed that kidnapping was a viable option, does that constitute a conspiracy to kidnap, or must the defendants have agreed that kidnapping was their chosen option that they would pursue?"

It is the answer to this question that foreman Bush will later tell the news media was the final push that convinced the jury to let the kidnappers off the hook.

Prosecutor Leiser wants the jury to be told, "The defendants could consider options and one of them could be kidnapping. If you find beyond a reasonable doubt that they reached an understanding as to that option, then you could find them guilty of that crime. . . . The fact that you're looking at various options doesn't negate the possibility that you reached an understanding or an agreement as to one."

Defense attorney Markham says, "They're asking . . . if you agree that it's a viable option, is that an offense? It clearly is not an offense. . . ." Markham's point is the height of sophistry.

After arguing with Leiser, Judge Ellis says he will tell the jury this: "Mere discussion of something as an option would not constitute a conspiracy to kidnap. However, if the option is discussed and then agreed upon that they would do it, then the crime is made out."

Markham demands the judge change the word "discussion" to "agreement." Markham has repeated to the jury over and over that the defendants were merely discussing kidnapping, not agreeing to do it. Now, he wants the jury told that even if the defendants went beyond mere discussion and agreed to kidnap, kidnapping has to be the only option they chose to pursue.

Judge Ellis finally puts it to the jury this way: "It is not enough for the defendants to agree or reach an understanding that kidnapping is a viable option. . . . They must arrive at some agreement or understanding to kidnap Lewis du Pont Smith or Andrea Diano."

The jury takes less than an hour after that to acquit all the defendants. Foreman Bush later tells the news media the jury was divided, but that it was the judge's answers which brought them around.

Marc Bush tells the *Philadelphia Inquirer,* "I felt badly for the family. I have a certain amount of sympathy for Newbold because I know he wanted to make it a cohesive family again." Bush tells the *Washington Post,* "I know how I'd feel if something like that happened to my family."

♦ ♦ ♦

Immediately after the verdict, Judge Ellis takes the unusual step of commenting on the case for the record.

"The principle for which the government advocated in this case has certainly been vindicated, which is to say that it doesn't matter whether it's a father trying to kidnap a son, or something else; if it's kidnapping, it's kidnapping.

"A reasonable citizen might ask, however, was that really what this case was about? Was this case about a federal criminal kidnapping, or was it about a tragic rift between a father and a son?" he asks rhetorically.

He disregards the evidence he had just heard about Newbold's seven-year vendetta against his son Lewis, that included Newbold's having his son declared mentally incompetent, breaking into his son's house, trying to destroy his son's marriage, having his son's wife indicted on bogus criminal charges, and hiring thugs to kidnap him, who did not rule out the possibility that Lewis might be killed.

"Or was it a tragic rift between a father and a son, who, for reasons unclear to the court, having to do with their personalities, their lives together, their relationship, profess great love for one another, but somehow seem not to be able to rely on that love to bridge the gap that grew up between them as a result of a difference in life views, a difference in views between a father and a son. And it is terribly tragic. And it is true that if the jury had found that there was an agreement to kidnap, that there is no question that that would have been a crime, and that is a crime for which they would have been punished."

Belying the real reason for his wrongheaded decision to keep Lewis from testifying, the judge pronounces, "I was particularly distressed to learn that the father and the son would really be testifying against one another, perhaps, in this case. That would have been especially regrettable had it been necessary to occur. As it happened, his testimony was neither relevant, and if relevant was cumulative, and wasn't necessary. But it would have been particularly tragic."

Judge Ellis goes on, "I suppose the bottom line is that the principle for which the government was advocating is a principle that really doesn't need a trial to be vindicated; it's a principle that ought to be clear to anyone. Nothing in the jury's verdict justifies or excuses any parent from trying to kidnap a child they believe is involved in some kind of cult, political activity, criminal activity, or other kind of activity. It does not justify a kidnapping, and the government should act with dispatch and effectivness in seeking to prosecute and halt such action."

Then, revealing his sympathy with Newbold Smith, Ellis rambles on. "What matters more than anything else—and I think you know this, Mr. Smith, and everyone else in here knows this—what matters more than anything else is your relationship. . . . You can't control his life. All you can do is tell him what any father would, give him advice, but it's his life."

Judge Ellis even chastises Lewis du Pont Smith, the intended kidnap victim, whom he denied a chance to tell his side of the story. "And I would hope that the young Mr. Smith would realize that no political belief he has, nothing he wants to do in life, is any more important than his relationship with his father. That doesn't mean he abandons or gives up things, but it means he accepts his father, too; accepts his father as having different views about some things, and that he realizes that his relationship and his love for his father is something that should take second place to nothing."

Ellis next excoriates the government, for even bringing charges against the would-be kidnappers. "It might have been worthwhile to call Mr. Smith into an office in a suitably somber way and say, 'Look, Mr. Smith, if you attempt to kidnap, or kidnap your son, you will be prosecuted under the federal law to the fullest extent. Make no mistake about that,'. . . rather than to spend a great deal of effort and time in watching what essentially amounted to 'the gang that couldn't shoot straight.' " This despite the fact that Newbold had been told numerous times that kidnapping was illegal, yet still conspired to have it done.

Kelly, the man who will kidnap anyone if the price is right, and who boasted on the very tapes Judge Ellis had just listened to, that he could talk his way out of any kidnapping charge, gets a slap on the wrist from the judge. "Mr. Kelly, I don't know where matters stand with you, but this trial ought to be a clear message to you that under no circumstances is it ever justified to snatch, lift, or pull anybody off the street against their will, however wacky you may think their views are, whatever activities they may be doing. . . . One man's cult is another man's community, however wacky you or I may think that is."

Kelly once again has escaped punishment for plotting to commit a violent crime.

Ellis treats Moore, whose violent rantings dominated the tapes, as if he were just a juvenile delinquent. "Mr. Moore, some of the things you said on the tape were positively silly. They were ridiculous. You're a mature person, and you should start acting like one. It's one thing to be a private investigator; it's quite another thing to be somebody out there fomenting illegal activity, or close to it.

"You came within an inch of being convicted here, and you should take it very seriously." Ellis is speaking to a man who for years treated his law enforcement powers as a license to do whatever he wants, whether within the law or outside the law. "You're obviously a person of ability and competence, and you've obviously served ably and with distinction in law enforcement. There are plenty of things you can do in law enforcement, but one of them is not to contemplate illegal activity."

Then to Kelly's legal adviser "Biker Bob" Point, whose advice to commit illegalities would be grounds for disbarment: "Mr. Point, you're a member of the bar. Of all the people, you should have stood up at the very outset and said, 'I don't want to hear any more discussion of kidnapping. I don't want to hear any more discussion of wetwork. I don't want to hear any more discussion of any illegal activity. I will not stand for it.' "

Finally, revealing his own bias, Ellis says, "It may be, ultimately, that the jury . . . may have felt to some extent, as the court does, that fundamentally this was a tragic, tragic rift between a father and a son, and they simply held the government to a very high standard on the proof."

Prosecutor Larry Leiser later tells the waiting press, "I still think Doug Poppa is a hero."

But now, the conspirators leave the courtroom as free men.

APPENDIX

International Efforts to Free Lyndon LaRouche

Since the jailing of American statesman Lyndon LaRouche in January 1989, there have been extraordinary efforts to free him from prison, ranging from a petition to President Bill Clinton, to LaRouche's 2255/ Rule 33 habeas corpus motion, to diplomatic efforts before the CSCE, the United Nations Human Rights Commission and the Organization of American States.

An Appeal to President Clinton

A letter, printed below, to President Bill Clinton seeking the freedom of Lyndon LaRouche, has been signed by over 1,000 distinguished persons from all around the world, a small portion of whom are listed here, since it began circulating after Mr. Clinton's election in November 1992.

Dear President Clinton:
In the course of your election campaign, and following your election as the President of the United States, you pledged to bring about a change in American policy.

We welcome this intent and wish you courage and stead-fastness for this difficult task.

We call upon you to take a first step in this direction: To end a crying injustice—see to it that Lyndon LaRouche is immediately set free and exonerated.

Lyndon LaRouche, who is innocent, has been incar-cerated as a political prisoner in the federal prison in Rochester, Minnesota since January 1989. He committed no crime; his sentencing and imprisonment were the result of years-long slanders and persecutions by forces of the Reagan-Bush administration, in combination with the media and private organizations, as well as forces of the secret services of formerly communist states.

Over 1,000 prominent jurists from all over the world have protested publicly against this abuse of justice, in the course of which LaRouche and a number of his associ-ates were supposed to be eliminated as an undesired opposition. Hundreds of parliamentarians and other prominent personalities from all over the world have joined this protest.

The LaRouche case was presented to the Human Rights Commission of the United Nations several times; U.N. Special Rapporteur Angelo Vidal D'Almeida Ribeiro included the case in his report last year to the U.N. Com-mission on Human Rights.

Since then, explosive new material has come to light documenting the political motivation behind this perse-cution. One U.S. court has, in fact, ruled that the trial had come into being as a result of "constructive fraud" on the part of the government.

We are outraged over the arrogance of the Bush government, which ignored all protests and appeals. Yet it was George Bush himself, who in 1988, i.e., before

LaRouche had been indicted in Alexandria, Va., declared in public that LaRouche belonged behind bars, thus, as Vice President, anticipating any legal procedure.

We, the undersigned, see ourselves as members of an international coalition to free Lyndon LaRouche. We appeal to you, President Clinton: Give a signal that you seriously mean to bring about change: Act! Take the necessary steps immediately to set LaRouche and his associates free!

I join the international coalition to free Lyndon LaRouche and endorse the above appeal.

Titles for identification purposes only.

EUROPE—ARMENIA: Haik Babookhanian, deputy, Yerevan City Parliament; Hrant Kachatrian, member of Parliament and Supreme Soviet; V. Kazarian, deputy, Yerevan City Parliament; Igor Muradian, member of Parliament and Supreme Soviet **AUSTRIA:** Dr. Marijan Brajinovic, Bd. member, Austrian-Croatian Society; Prof. Dr. Kurt Ebert, vice dir., Inst. for Legal History, Innsbruck Univ.; Farid Hanna, perm. rep. to U.N. office, Vienna; Dr. Ludwig Hoffmann-Rumerstein, attorney; Prof. Dr. Hans Klecatsky, former Minister of Justice; Prof. Dr. Hans Koechler, pres., Int'l Progress Org. **BELGIUM:** Nicole Delpérée, gerontology law expert **CROATIA:** Srecko Jurdana, journalist **CZECH REPUBLIC:** Ladislav Boucek, journalist **DENMARK:** Fritz Hermann, chmn., Mutual Org. for Farming (LFO) **FRANCE:** Jean-Marie Alexandre, deputy, Euro. Parliament; Marie Jo Denys, deputy, Euro. Parliament; Roger Garaudy, writer; Mayor Marcel Le Bihan, Pompey; Gen. Jean-Gabriel Revault d'Allonnes (ret.); Joseph Rozier, Bishop of Poitiers, nat'l pres., Pax Christi; Haroun Tazieff, volcanologist **GERMANY:** Helmut Eichinger, chmn., Assn. of German

Farmers (VDL); Lissy Groener, deputy, Euro. Parliament; Brig. Gen. Friedrich Wilhelm Grunewald (ret.); Ludwig Guettler, musician; Heinz Hildebrandt, deputy, Saxon-Anhalt Parliament; Brig. Gen. Heinz Karst (ret.); Ilse Luebben, deputy, Lower Saxony Parliament; Brig. Gen. Jobst Rohkamm (ret.); Christine Scheel, deputy, Bavarian State Parliament; Brig. Gen. Paul A. Scherer (ret.), former chief, West German Military Intelligence; Sigrun Steinborn, deputy, Berlin Parliamentary Assembly; Vice Adm. Karl-Adolf Zenker (ret.) **HUNGARY:** Janos Denes, member of Parliament; Dr. Janos Gojak, theologian, Budapest; Dr. Tibor Kovats, Bd. member, Assn. of Former Political Prisoners **ITALY:** Roberto Barzanti, vice pres., Euro. Parliament; Prof. Giulio Basetti-Sani, OFM, Trento Cultural Inst.; Msgr. Luigi Bettazzi, past pres., Pax Christi; Maria Luisa Cassanmagnago Cerretti, deputy, Euro. Parliament; Roberto Formigoni, deputy, Euro. Parliament; deputy, Italian Parliament; Francesco Guidolin, deputy, Euro. Parliament; Antonio Iodice, deputy, Euro. Parliament; Carmine Mancuso, member of the Senate; Raffaele Morini, pres., Enrico Mattei Study Center; Nico Perrone, law faculty, Bari Univ.; Flaminio Piccoli, member of the Senate; Domenico Romano, deputy, Italian Parliament; Giovanni Russo Spena, member of Parliament; Luigi Vinci, member of the Senate **NETHERLANDS:** Stefan Metz, artistic dir., Orlando Festival, Amsterdam **POLAND:** Leszek Bialkowski, adviser, Trade Union "Solidarity 80"; Prof. Dr. Stephan Kurowski, Catholic Univ., Lublin **RUSSIA:** Y. Chernichenko, nat'l deputy, pres., Farmers' Party of Russia; Prof. Dr. Jakow Drabkin, dir., Research Ctr. for German History, Moscow; Viktor Kuzin, chmn., Human Rights Commission, Moscow Soviet; Vladimir Matveev, coordinator, Dem. Union,

Moscow; Prof. Dr. Taras Muranivsky, rector, Ukrainian Univ. in Moscow; Valeria Novodvorskaja, leader, Dem. Union party, Moscow; Sergei Pavlov, deputy, St. Petersburg Soviet; Alexei Pogorilyi, deputy, Moscow Soviet **SLOVAK REPUBLIC:** Mierova Spolocnost, "Peace Society" of Slovak Republic, Levice **SWEDEN:** Jadwiga-Helena Boral, founding member, Polish Solidarity movement; John Bouvin, member of Parliament **SWITZERLAND:** Ibrahim Salah **UKRAINE:** Pavlo Movchan, member of Parliament **UNITED KINGDOM:** John Bird, member, Euro. Parliament, Wolverhampton; Prof. Dr. Norbert Brainin, O.B.E., violinist, London,, England; Charles Gray, chmn., Int'l Bd. of Local Gov'ts, Glasgow, Scotland; Right Rev. Michael Hare-Duke, Bishop of St. Andrews, Perth, Scotland

IBERO-AMERICA—ARGENTINA: Arturo Frondizi, former President of Argentina; Mario Caponnetto, cardiologist; Sergio Ceron, journalist **BRAZIL:** Luiz Carlos Casagrande, state legislator, Rio Grande do Sul; Fernando Correa de Sa Benevides, journalist; Dom Manoel Pestana Filho, Bishop of Anapolis; Roberto Saturnino Braga, city councilman, Rio de Janeiro; Col. (ret.) Pedro Schirmer, editor, *Ombro a Ombro;* Helio Zawatski, pres., Rio Grande do Sul Cooperatives **COLOMBIA:** Ernesto Amezquita, pres., Nat'l Trial Lawyers Assn.; Jorge Carrillo, former Minister of Labor; Apolinar Garcia, secy. gen., Nat'l Agrarian Federation; Alfonso Gonzalez, member of Congress; Eduardo Kronfly, prof. of law; Edgar Eulises Torres, member of Congress; Gen. (ret.) Hernando Zuluaga **MEXICO:** Carlos Rafael Acosta Arvizu, member, Sonora state legislature; Octavio Elizalde, attorney; J.J. Gonzalez Gortazar, member of Congress; Jesus Gonzalez Schmall, nat'l coordinator, Forum of Democ-

racy and Doctrine; Juan Jaime Hernandez, PARM; Pablo
Emilio Madero, member of Congress; Jorge Moscoso,
member of Congress; Jose Ramirez Yanez, Mayor, Gomez
Farias, Jalisco; Adalberto Rosas, former state legislator,
Sonora; Cecilia Soto, member of Congress; Manuel Vil-
lagomez Rodriguez, pres., Fed. of Microindustries **PAN-
AMA:** Isabel Corro, pres., Assn. of Families of Victims
of Dec. 20, 1989 U.S. Invasion; Elmo Martinez Blanco,
former Minister of Industry and Commerce; Manuel Solis
Palma, former President of Panama **PERU:** Manuel Ger-
man Benza Pflucker, former member of Congress; Juan
Bernaola, secy. gen., Confed. of Workers of the Peruvian
Revolution; Felipe Oswaldo Bockos, former member of
Congress; Col. (ret.) Roberto Caceres Velasquez, member
of Congress; pres., Human Rts. Ctte; Rodrigo Cordova
Saona; Lino Cerna Manrique, former member of Con-
gress; Josmell Munoz, former member of the Senate;
Msgr. Alfredo Noriega Arce, S.J., Auxiliary Bishop of
Lima; Francisco Palomino Garcia, former Member of
Congress; Gen. (ret.) Julio German Parra Herrera, former
Minister of Transportation and Communication; Juan Re-
baza Carpio, former Minister of Fisheries; Francisco Vi-
darte Garcia, pres., Assn. of Nuclear Professionals, Nu-
clear Energy Institute **VENEZUELA:** Emil Guevara
Munoz, secy., int'l affairs, People's Electoral Movement;
Simon J. Pacheco, farm leader

   NORTH AMERICA: Jim Albright, past state pres.,
Alabama Bldg. Trades Council; Milton B. Allen, retired
judge, Baltimore, City Circuit Ct., MD; Ali Baghdadi,
editor, *Al-Bostaan Journal,* Chicago, IL; Almanina Bar-
bour, Esq., Philadelphia, PA; James Barnett, chmn., Coalition Black Trade Unionists, N.W. AL; Rev. Richard
Boone, former SCLC field coord., Ala. Cities Project;

Francis Boyle, prof. of law, Univ. of Illinois, Champaign;
George Branch, city councilman, Newark, NJ; Bernard
and Rose Mae Broussard, Starthrowers, LA; Frank Caligi-
uri Jr., Exec. Bd., UAW, Buffalo, NY; Rev. Ben Chavis,
civil rights leader and columnist, Cleveland, OH; Annie
Coleman, vice pres., Coalition of Black Trade Unionists,
CA; David A. Collins, City Council member, Buffalo, NY;
Paul Comiskey, S.J., pres., Prisoners' Rts. Assn.; Sylvia
Cox, exec. vice pres., Nat'l Assn. of Black Women Law-
yers; Gary Daniels, pres., Int'l Broth. Boilermakers Loc.
684, VA; Del. Clarence Davis, MD Gen. Assembly; John
W. DeCamp, former Nebraska State Senator; Joseph
Dickson, publisher, *Birmingham World;* Msgr. David I.
Dorsch, Archdiocese of Baltimore; Don Eret, former state
Senator, NE; Most Rev. Basil Filevich, Bishop of Sas-
katchewan; Rafael Flores, Bd. member, Hispanics for
Life, Los Angeles, CA; James M. Franklin, past pres.,
AFGE Loc. 421, Wash. DC; Josip Gamulin, pres., Cro-
atian Ctte. for Human Rights, Toronto; Justice William
C. Goodloe (ret.), Wash. State Supreme Court; Isador
Hampton, pres., UAW Loc. 835, MI; Ron Hampton, nat'l
dir., Nat'l Black Policemen's Assn.; Henry Helstoski, for-
mer U.S. Congressman, NJ; Fred Huenefeld, past pres.,
Nat'l Org. of Raw Materials; Sen. Jerry Jewell, state legis-
lature, AR; Jerrauld Jones, member, VA House of Dele-
gates, Norfolk, VA; Rev. Robert J.N. Jones, pres., Rich-
mond SCLC, VA; Rabbi Gerald Kaplan, Brooklyn, NY;
Kazimierz Kasperek, editor, *The Alliancer,* Cleveland,
OH; Clifford Kelly, former Chicago City Councilman;
Alex Kindy, member, Canadian Parliament, Ottawa; Rev.
Leon G. Lipscombe, Wash., DC; Rose-Marie Love, former
Cook County Commissioner, IL; Rev. Eugene Lumpkin,
San Francisco, CA; James J. Lumpkin, secy.-treas., ILA

Loc. 1458, VA; John Madrid, Bd. of Dir., Hispanics for
Life, Los Angeles, CA; Colman McCarthy, syndicated
columnist, Wash., DC; Art Minson, chmn., Pol. Action
Ctte., Akron NAACP, OH; State Sen. Theo Walker Mitch-
ell, SC; Valencia Mohammed, at-large member, Wash.,
DC School Bd.; John Monks, chmn., Veterans Affairs
Ctte., Oklahoma House of Reps.; Dr. Abdul Alim Muham-
mad, Minister of Health, Nation of Islam; Siah Nyanseor,
chmn., African Anti-Malthusian League, Atlanta, GA;
George Perdue, member, Alabama House of Reps.; Vel
Phillips, former Wisconsin Secretary of State; Rev. Regi-
nald Pitcher, pres., Baton Rouge SCLC, LA; John Ram-
sey, pres., Asphalt Workers Loc. 889, Newark, NJ; Clin-
ton Roberson, pres., African American Lawyers Assn.;
William P. Robinson, Jr., attorney, Norfolk, VA; Ed Sal-
dana, Mex. Am. League Against Crime, Los Angeles,
CA; Greg Schumacher, farm leader, SD; Rev. Marshall
Shepard, past pres., Progressive Nat'l Baptist Convention;
John Shike, ed. and pub., *Voice of Freedom,* Houston, TX;
Barbara Lett Simmons, pres., Wash., DC Dem. Women's
Club; Rev. Glen Staples, vice moderator, Immanuel Mis-
sionary Baptist Assn., Wash., DC; Fr. Thomas Tou, pres.,
Chinese Assn. of Montreal; George Vaughn, Dem. Party
whip, Oklahoma House of Reps; Rev. Wade Watts, past
pres., Oklahoma NAACP; Steven Whitehead, pres., Ports-
mouth Central Labor Council, VA; Ervin Williams, pres.,
IBT Loc. 822, Norfolk, VA; Rev. Hosea Williams, DeKalb
County Commissioner, GA; James Wilson, vice pres.,
Watts NAACP, CA; Wyatt Wilson, pres., LA Coalition for
Prison Reform; Nadine Winters, former member, Wash.,
DC City Council; Rev. Canon Joseph Francis Xavier, An-
glican Church of Canada
    AFRICA, ASIA and AUSTRALIA: Kassim Ahmad,

author, Malaysia; Denis Collins, member, Legis. Assembly, N. Terr., Australia; Mohideen Abdul Kader, attorney, Malaysia; Fr. Augustine Liu, Superior, Franciscan Friars, Taipei, ROC; Joseph Minko, accountant, African Reconstruction Forum, Gabon; Gobinda Mukhoty, pres., Confed. Indian Consumer Orgs., India; Kuldip Nayar, chmn., Citizens for Democracy, India; Ni Yuxian, leader, Liberal Dem. Party, China; I.F. Xavier, dir., Home for Human Rights for Sri Lanka; H.G. Ward, governor, Int'l Policy Forum, South Africa

LaRouche Case Brought Before CSCE

Ramsey Clark Warns About U.S. Rights Violations at 1990 CSCE Conference

Below are excerpts from a speech given by former U.S. Attorney General Ramsey Clark, one of LaRouche's attorneys for his appeal of his conviction. Clark spoke on the LaRouche case in Copenhagen, Denmark in June 1990, at a conference of the Commission on Security and Cooperation in Europe (CSCE). In 1991, the international Commission to Investigate Human Rights Violations followed up on Mr. Clark's speech, by again focusing international attention on the LaRouche case at a Conference on the Human Dimension of the CSCE in Moscow, Russia.

Speaking before a packed audience in Copenhagen, Denmark on June 21, 1990, former U.S. Attorney General Ramsey Clark warned that the conference on Human Rights Violations being held there by the Conference on Security and Cooperation in Europe (CSCE) should carefully study the pattern of massive violations of human rights in the United States, which has gone hand-in-hand with the increased degradation of the growing ranks of the nation's poor people—many of whom are darker-skinned.

Clark's trip was sponsored by the Schiller Institute's Commission to Investigate Human Rights Violations, a non-governmental organization which is urging the CSCE to take up the case of Lyndon LaRouche. Also in Copenhagen urging consideration of the LaRouche case was LaRouche's wife, Helga Zepp-LaRouche, who is a leading political figure in her own right in Germany.

At Copenhagen, Clark explained that he has no political identification with LaRouche and disagrees with many things LaRouche has said, "but I would defend to the near-death his right to say it."

U.S. Prison System Is Intolerable

But before going into the LaRouche case, Clark spoke about many other things happening in and around the United States, "because I think it's the only context in which you can understand what the LaRouche case is about."

"We have a prison population of a dimension that you can hardly believe in Europe," he said. "Our prison population in the United States right now exceeds the population of the city of Copenhagen. ... Our prison population . . . is a multiple of up to 20 times, and not less than ten, of any country in Western Europe, and as far as we know, not less than ten of any country in Eastern Europe. We have five states that have a higher prison population than the total [prison] population in South Africa. Our prisons are brutalizing places. They manufacture crime. Our prison population is the biggest growth industry in the United States—15-25 percent a year increase. Construction of prisons is one of the biggest businesses.

"Do you want to know who's in those prisons?" Clark continued. "Overwhelmingly, poor, young—very young, black, Hispanic, other minority men. . . . They're only slightly different from the homeless in the United States. . . . The people who live without any shelter in the United States exceed, again, the population of Copenhagen." The current estimate, he said, is about 850,000 sleeping outside on any given night.

Clark also cited U.S. injustices abroad:

● "Grenada was the biggest news story by all surveys in the United States in 1983, and nobody even knows that they may hang 14 people on one day in Grenada, financed by the United States. . . . The symbolism is powerful. It is: If you defy the United States in its own lake, we'll invade and we will kill, and will indict the survivors, and they'll be hung."

● "What about the thousands killed in Jakarta [Indonesia] in 1965 who were simply listed by the CIA—just listed. How good was that information? What was the charge? Communism!

● "While that goes on, you see the National Endowment for Democracy. Another one of these euphemisms—it ought to be called the National Endowment for Destruction of Democracy, because it's U.S. funding for the subversion of democratic processes in other countries by the expenditure of U.S. electoral knowledge and U.S. money to . . . install leadership in a foreign country of U.S. choice.

"How many elections in East Europe involve activity by the National Endowment for Democracy? Does that concern this conference? It ought to! It's done the same thing in the Philippines to support Marcos when he was there; it's done the same thing in Salvador for Duarte and Cristiani. Watch Liberia—where people have lived under a brutal military dictatorship for a decade—but the United States doesn't express outrage when Master Sergeant Samuel K. Doe murdered Tolbert in the President's mansion! Dragged his son out of the French embassy to kill him in the streets in front of the embassy! Took the leadership of the government down to the beach at Monrovia, tied them to stakes in the morning and let them wilt through the day before blasting their heads off that night!"

● Clark recounted his trip to Panama in January 1990, following the U.S. invasion, and how after the U.S. military told him that only 83 Panamanians had been killed, he went out to the "Garden of Peace" cemetery and discovered a mass grave of hundreds of bodies wrapped in green bags—and that was only one of many mass graves.

● Clark noted that the "Thornburgh Doctrine" actually began in December 1986 with an Executive Order signed by President Ronald Reagan authorizing kidnappings overseas. "You ought to pay attention," he warned the Europeans, "you could be kidnapped right from this room, under U.S. law, by U.S. agents."

Method to the Madness

Returning to what is happing on U.S. territory, Clark explained that "there's method to this madness. Why is it that virtually every major black elected official has been the subject of a criminal investigation or a prosecution? . . . Why is [Washington, D.C. Mayor] Marion Barry on trial right now? . . . At the same time, there have been several columns written that a principal associate of the Attorney General [Richard Thornburgh] . . . is permitted to resign and return to Pennsylvania under charges that he was using cocaine. And no investigation and no prosecution.

"Political control! You talk about American democracy, and I tell you it's a plutocracy—without question. . . . Money absolutely dominates politics in the United States. Never doubt it. Hundreds of millions of dollars is going to our elections. That's the way we do it. . . . Very few people in the United States have name recognition. I'm not talking about issues—you don't know their names, much less what they stand for! There's no discussion of the issues—it's money, pure and simple."

The Two Parties Are Actually One

"Then you come to someone like Lyndon LaRouche, and you see what the problem is. We have always had what we call a two-party system. It's been called the genius of American politics. It really fools you. I'll tell you—I'm a slow learner and I admit that—but I was 40 years old before it occurred to me that this two-party system wasn't the greatest thing since apple pie. Then one day I realized, there's no difference! . . .

"The two-party system is a one-party system with two names, and it's a personality contest. . . . Then a Lyndon LaRouche comes along and offers an alternative in politics. Whether it's good or bad, he is a danger to the system, just as black elected officials are. . . . You see years and years of prejudicial publicity, and then you see certain clues: He is rushed to trial. . . . If you take the biggest drug cases, 45 of the major dealers in one case, it won't go to trial in 15 months, I guarantee you. Take Noriega, with all the fanfare. How long has he been in custody now? Since January. When does he go to trial? Maybe next January. Lyndon LaRouche—you've got to indict him three weeks before an election.

"I was in the Department of Justice for eight years," Clark continued. "We never indicted a political figure before an election. . . . Because if you do, then how do the people know whether you're using the prosecution power to manipulate the political process? And there he is, indicted, three weeks before the election! You couldn't wait! He was on the ballot in 20 states. . . . He had a right to get as many votes as he could. He could have gotten quite a few votes—a million, two million, who knows. . . ."

As for the trial against LaRouche in Alexandria, Va., the rigged jury selection alone was proof that "there was no intention of having a fair trial. . . . You make three sentences for five years each to impose a 15-year sentence on a man who's 66 years old. To destroy a political movement—obviously."

In conclusion, Clark admonished, "If you want to have change in the United States, it will have to come through the policial process. . . . Unless you can wrench that free from plutocracy that absolutely controls with an iron hand that essentially one-party system, you won't have change. And that's what the Lyndon LaRouche case is about."

U.N. Human Rights Commission Hears About Crimes Against LaRouche

February 1991 IPO Address Sought Investigation of Role of Kissinger and Bush in LaRouche Imprisonment

On February 28, 1991, Warren A.J. Hamerman, speaking as an official representative of the International Progress Organization (IPO), addressed a full plenary session of the 47th Session on Human Rights of the United Nations in Geneva, Switzerland on the Lyndon LaRouche case. Hamerman called for an immediate investigation by the Special Rapporteur of the U.N. and the Human Rights Commission, into the frame-up prosecution of LaRouche by the U.S. government, that was in violation of both the Declaration on the Elimination of all Forms of Intolerance and of Discrimination based on Religion or Belief proclaimed by the General Assembly in 1981 and the Universal Declaration of Human Rights proclaimed by the General Assembly in 1948. The full text of Mr. Hamerman's speech follows.

Mr. Chairman:

I wish to urgently call the attention of the nations of the world to the fact that there is an increasing pattern inside the United States of individuals and associations being targetted, prosecuted and harassed by government because of their political and philosophic beliefs. This infringement against the dignity and equality inherent in all human beings stands in violation of both the Declaration on the Elimination of all Forms of Intolerance and of Discrimination based on Religion or Belief proclaimed by the General Assembly resolution 36/55 of 25 November 1981 and the Universal Declaration of Human Rights proclaimed by General Assembly Resolution 217 A (III) of 10 December 1948.

While the U.S. Constitution and laws contain model language of protections, in practice the actions and deeds of the U.S. and state governments have singled out individuals and associations whose philosphic and political beliefs place them in opposition to America's ever more assertive policies internationally and domestically.

Such politically or philosphically motivated targetting of a governmental "Enemies' List" is documented in the following instances:

1. Government operations against Dr. Martin Luther King, Jr., his followers and among minority elected officials who raise too many hopes for economic and social justice at a time that the government is obsessed with scarcity and austerity.

2. Government overt and covert actions against those who challenge grand-scale, neo-colonialist adventures against the developing sector as in Vietnam, Panama and now the Persian Gulf.

3. Excessive prosecutions against those who struggle for life principles against wholesale euthanasia and abortions.

4. Massive judicial abuses against the political and publishing movement associated with Lyndon H. LaRouche, Jr., the American politician and physical economist who has been a *political prisoner* for over two years.

Lyndon LaRouche is the founder and leader of a philosophic and political association with defined beliefs which he has staunchly struggled to propagate. These beliefs center around the right of all peoples—especially in the Third World and among the poor everywhere—to development and economic justice. Mr. LaRouche has fought for the belief that economics and morality cannot be separated since all human beings are equally the children of God, created in his image to be fruitful, multiply and have dominion over the earth (Genesis I:26-28). Mr. LaRouche has fought to introduce these beliefs into the political process and has met with a hostile and furious opposition to his beliefs from those in government who instead were promoting genocide, economic injustice, disproportionate misery and social disadvantage for the developing sector and poor.

I call upon the Special Rapporteur and Commission to fully investigate these increasing infringements of the rights and freedoms of "thought, conscience and belief" and the principle of "equality before the law," as mandated by the Declaration.

In the case of Government actions against LaRouche and his associates—including the shutting down of publications, banning a free political action committee, large-scale police raids involving hundreds of militarized and armed personnel, seizing of bank accounts and records through secret procedures later to be found fraudulent by independent courts, and excessive prison terms of "life sentences" for a number of people—there are specific violations against, at least, the following aspects of the Declaration:

1. "The right to write, issue and disseminate relevant publications according to one's beliefs."

2. "The right to collect and receive voluntary financial and other contributions from individuals and institutions."

3. "The freedom to either individually or in community with others and in public or private to manifest one's belief."

4. "The freedom to enjoy and propagate that belief in all fields of civil, economic, political, social and cultural life."

5. "The right to establish and maintain appropriate charitable or humanitarian institutions."

6. "The right to establish and maintain communication with individuals and communities at the national and international level."

Nearly 1,000 prominent American jurists and human rights scholars have publicly condemned the abuses by the U.S. government in the LaRouche case. Among these distinguished individuals are two board members of the IPO—former Austrian Minister of Justice Hans Klecatsky and former U.S. Attorney General Ramsey Clark.

During 1990, the IPO endorsed the complaint of Human Rights violations in the United States of America which was filed on 26 January 1990 by the International Commission to Investigate Human Rights Violations and Mrs. Helga Zepp-LaRouche. The president of the IPO, Dr. Hans Koechler of Austria, personally delivered the complaint along with a supplemental Memorandum by Dr. Hans Klecatsky to the deputy director of the Human Rights Commission in Geneva.

At the parallel CSCE conference on the "Human Dimension" which took place from June 5-29, 1990 in Copenhagen, Ramsey Clark declared that the indictment of Lyndon LaRouche, following years of press vilification for his beliefs, was a government attempt to use the "prosecution power to manipulate the political process." Mr. Clark stated:

"Lyndon LaRouche was indicted three weeks before a presidential election. I was in the Department of Justice for eight years. We never indicted a political figure before an election. . . . LaRouche was on the ballot in twenty states. What's going to happen to his campaign? Nobody says he was going to get elected, but he had a right to run."

In the IPO's supplemental Memorandum to the 1503 Human Rights Violations Complaint, Prof. Klecatsky identified the following areas of Human Rights concern in the LaRouche case:

1. The incredible rush to trial within 38 days after indictment.

2. The stacking of the initial jury pool and final jury with government employees of the FBI, Department of Justice, CIA and the emergency government "secret" apparatus which LaRouche had widely criticized.

3. The barring of evidence at trial which could prove government frame-up and harassment. The defense charged that the government had itself manufactured the "economic crimes" by shutting down three LaRouche-associated firms through a forced bankruptcy. Ten months after LaRouche was locked away in prison, another federal judge found that the 1987 involuntary bankruptcy forced by the government was indeed unlawful, done in "bad faith," and through a "fraud on the court" in a secret ex parte proceeding.

4. The issuance of effective "death sentences" for crimes which most nations in the world regard as minor civil or administrative infractions. The 68-year-old

LaRouche is currently serving a 15-year sentence. Various of his associates in separate state trials were given sentences of 77 years, 86 years, 41, 45 and 46 years.

Such a pattern of basic human rights violations is characteristic of the "retaliatory justice" which governments reserve for those whom they deem politically or philosophically dangerous.

Yet, often it is the non-conventional "dissident" idea which can solve problems more humanely and efficiently than state policy.

For instance, in 1975 Mr. LaRouche travelled to Baghdad, Iraq where he proposed a program for the "Greening of the Desert" through a large-scale water and economic development regional project based upon cooperation between the Iraqi, Israeli and Palestinian peoples (as well as the others in the area.) After initial positive reactions among Arab, Israeli and Palestinian people, the very same individuals in the U.S. government who later went after him judicially opposed the proposal. Were it adopted, the world today would have seen the desert bloom, instead of storm.

I call upon the Commission and Special Rapporteur to investigate these matters with thoroughness and speed.

Documentation exists to suggest that those in government who wished to suppress the beliefs of Lyndon LaRouche and his associates misused their access to state power in order to silence the propagation of beliefs it judged as "extreme" or "threatening" to prevailing policy trends. Two such individuals are:

1. Former Secretary of State Dr. Henry Kissinger, who opposed Mr. LaRouche's Mideast Regional Development and new World Economic Order beliefs, and subsequently initiated a large government Task Force to develop a case against Mr. LaRouche. (This is documented through a series of signed letters by Mr. Kissinger and his attorney to then-FBI Director William Webster in 1982, and the minutes of a January 12, 1983 meeting of the President's Foreign Intelligence Advisory Board (PFIAB) meeting.)

2. Current President George Bush, who refuses to release to Mr. LaRouche's defense team thousands of pages of exculpatory documents which the government acknowledges that they have but cannot release because they are part of a "national Security Repository." (This is documented through a series of signed letters between myself and George Bush on October 11 and 20, 1989, the White House response of October 30, 1989, and various affidavits by FBI and justice Department officials.)

I wish to thank the chairman for this opportunity to speak and urge that the investigation into these matters be guided by the desire to find the truth about these grave threats to human liberty.

At U.N. Subcommission on Prevention of Discrimination 1991 Session

On Aug. 9, 1991, legal experts from all over the world sitting on the United Nations Organization Subcommission on Prevention of Discrimination and Protection of Minorities, heard the details of the case of discrimination against Lyndon LaRouche and his associates in the United States. The subcommission is part of the United Nations Commission on Human Rights. Warren Hamerman, speaking on behalf of the International Progress Organization (IPO), a Non-Governmental Organization in consultative status with the United Nations Economic and Social Council, presented the LaRouche case to the subcommission, at its 43rd session in Geneva, Switzerland. Below is the full text of Hamerman's presentation on behalf of the IPO:

Mr. Chairman,

Major human rights violations are now ongoing in the *United States* against the freedom of thought and conscience for all individuals, their freedom to form associations, and their freedom to manifest those beliefs in practice and teaching. These abuses are occurring solely for the reason that certain beliefs have been targetted by the government and power structures as politically "not correct," and the proponents of these beliefs have been vilified in the media and subjected to sustained government repression. In particular instances where the beliefs champion the rights of developing sector populations, beliefs which are out-of-step with the prevailing policy of an imposed world order, the proponents of these beliefs have been singled out for special persecution. Thus, my remarks today will consolidate references to the agenda item on the new international economic order, as well as on the elimination of all forms of intolerance for belief.

'American Dreyfus Affair'

The premier instance of U.S. government persecution for purely philosophical beliefs centered around championing the rights of the developing sector, as distinguished from religious beliefs per se, is the complex of cases involving the American political prisoner *Lyndon H. LaRouche, Jr.*, whose case has been referred to by one of Europe's most distinguished authorities on international law as "The American Dreyfus Affair." LaRouche is the founder of a broad-based philosophical and political association which has been attacked over a sustained period of time with the full force of government repression, simply because those in power find his beliefs a direct challenge to the delusion that a homogeneous new "world order" can be imposed from the top down.

LaRouche has been a political prisoner for over two and a half years. He was imprisoned virtually simultaneously with the inauguration of President George Bush, his longstanding political adversary. Two of his appeals to the U.S. Supreme Court—one a *habeas corpus* writ and one on an appeal of his conviction—were denied without his even being granted the right to present his case before that body. He has no prospect for release within the average human lifespan, as the nearly 70-year-old LaRouche is serving a 15-year sentence with the earliest release date coming between mid-1997 and 1999. Thus, he has been given an effective *slow death sentence* for matters which other nations would consider minor administrative or civil infractions.

Over the past five years, 50 leaders of the LaRouche political movement across the United States have been indicted, of whom 18 have been convicted in trials which are in violation of international fair trial standards, and 11 were jailed. As with LaRouche himself, many of his leading associates were given excessive sentences out of all proportion to the alleged crime. In a series of related prosecutions in the state of Virginia, for instance, four men and one woman—all in their mid-40s—were given sentences of 77 years, 39 years, 38 years, 34 years, and 25 years respectively.

In addition to these individual persons, five companies related to publishing writings or expressing beliefs associated with LaRouche were indicted. A nationally distributed newspaper with a circulation of more than

150,000 copies per issue (*New Solidarity*) was seized by the government in 1987 and shut down. An internationally respected scientific journal and association (the *Fusion Energy Foundation*) with an American subscribers list of 100,000 alone, had its offices padlocked and its journal banned by the government four years ago. Two publishing and distributing companies of literature promoting LaRouche's beliefs (*Campaigner Publications* and *Caucus Distributors, Inc.*), which published and circulated millions of copies of leaflets, pamphlets, and books promoting Third World development among Americans, had their offices seized, their presses stopped, and their stocks of literature confiscated through an extraordinary government decree known as a "forced bankruptcy." This was the first occasion in U.S. history that the government utilized this mechanism against publishing and political entities. Furthermore, in the same time period the government forced a free political action committee (the *National Democratic Policy Committee*) to cease functioning by imposing a draconian fine of $5 million on the small political action committee—an economic death sentence. One individual who contributed a substantial amount of money to promote LaRouche's beliefs—Lewis du Pont Smith—was dragged into court and found to be mentally incompetent for holding those beliefs and barred from controlling his own finances or even marrying by court order.

'Economic Crimes'

In their trial LaRouche and his associates were not charged with overt philosophic and political crimes but convicted of state-created "economic crimes" which the government itself had manufactured through the aforementioned bankruptcy. First, the government shut down the publishing firms through the unprecedented "involuntary bankruptcy." Then, they turned around and convicted LaRouche of failing to repay the debts of the out-of-existence companies, as well as hiding information from the government's Internal Revenue Service for the same unpayable money. Ten months *after* LaRouche was locked away in prison, the "forced bankruptcy" action by the government was found by an independent court headed by one of the most prominent bankruptcy judges in the country to be (1) an *illegal* action; (2) done in "*bad faith*" by the government; and (3) obtained by the government doing a "*constructive fraud on the court.*" Nevertheless, LaRouche sits in federal prison today serving his slow death sentence.

During the 47th session of the U.N. Commission on Human Rights, the International Progress Organization brought this case to the floor of the plenary session on Feb. 28, 1991 as a major instance of human rights violation because of discrimination against a belief. On May 31, 1991, the IPO filed a Petition to the Secretary General of the United Nations under the provisions of Resolution 1503.

Calls for LaRouche's Release

Since the IPO raised the LaRouche case at the February plenary session, hundreds of the world's most prominent and respected jurists, religious leaders, human rights experts, and political figures have filed documentation with the U.N. Human Rights Commission here in Geneva urging that the U.N. intervene into the *ongoing* violation of human rights. The expert documentation attesting to the importance of the IPO's complaint has come from the following:

- Leaders of virtually every major legal and civil rights association in the United States including the American Civil Liberties Union, the American Trial Lawyers Association, the National Association of Criminal Defense Attorneys, the American Bar Association's Human Rights Committee, the Mexican-American Legal Defense and Education Fund, and the National Association for the Advancement of Colored People.

- Religious leaders from around the world, including nearly 70 Catholic bishops and cardinals, 600 Protestant ministers, the leaders of a half-dozen American black Christian denominations, and the National Council of Islamic Affairs.

- From South America, 16 members of the Peruvian Congress have signed a communication deploring the abuses of human rights in the LaRouche case. Over 100 Senators and Congressmen from seven different Latin American nations had previously signed a statement denouncing the human rights abuses in the LaRouche case.

- From across Europe, several hundred jurists, politicians, artists, and religious leaders have added their names to the growing list of those concerned with this case.

- Finally, 10 U.S. Congressmen, seven U.S. Senators, and state legislators from five states, have urged the Human Rights Commission to take action in this case.

LaRouche's Policies

It is necessary to make a brief summary indication of LaRouche's beliefs because they directly set the context for vital information central to the Agenda item on the new international economic order. LaRouche's beliefs center around three themes which he has aggressively struggled to introduce into the political arena:

1. His promotion of science, technology, and physical economic progress for the developing nations. He has proposed large-scale economic infrastructure and development projects for the very areas in Africa, Asia, the Middle East, Latin America, and Eastern Europe which the international banking community has written off.

2. His opposition to the "demographic political warfare," or "Malthusian genocide," to use a more direct term, which has been waged against the Third World.

3. His opposition to the proliferation of a counterculture and his promotion instead of a revival of classical culture which celebrates the sacred dignity of all men and women as equally the children of God.

This brings me to my concluding contribution. Over the past few years, the U.S. government has declassified a series of National Security memoranda from the period of 1974-77 in which the U.S. government declared the movement for a New World Economic Order as a "national security" threat to the United States. This not only sheds light on why Mr. LaRouche was targetted in particular, but why major human rights violations with respect to Agenda items 7 and 13 have occurred.

The critical document is National Security Study Memorandum 200, "The Implications of Worldwide Population Growth for U.S. Security and Overseas Interest," which was written in 1974 by National Security Advisers Henry Kissinger and Brent Scowcroft.

One of the major concerns of NSSM 200 was to

check the spread of beliefs which encouraged a New World Economic Order with increasing population growth in the Third World. The document cites 13 "key countries" in which there is a special U.S. "strategic interest" in imposing population control and diminishing economic expectations.

Two years after NSSM 200 was written, in May of 1976, the National Security Council of the United States released a related memorandum reporting on progress. This report was forwarded to then-CIA director George Bush. This report, recently declassified, stated that it was in U.S. national security interests to eradicate "wishful thinking that economic development will solve" the problems in the developing sector.

I submit to the world community represented here that it is precisely opposition to the "wishful thinking" of a New World Economic Order which is at the center of the major human rights violations which are the subject of Agenda items 13 and 7.

In 1992, U.N. Commission Asks U.S. to Respond to Charges of Rights Violations Against LaRouche

The U.S. government was asked, in a report February 7, 1992, to respond to charges that it violated the human rights of Lyndon LaRouche by United Nations official Angelo Vidal D'Almeida Ribeiro, the U.N. Special Rapporteur who is mandated to investigate compliance with the "Declaration Based on the Elimination of All Forms of Intolerance and of Discrimination Based on Religion or Belief." The extraordinary charges were included in a report to the 48th plenary session of the United Nations Human Rights Commission in Geneva, Switzerland.

"According to information received, United States citizen Mr. Lyndon H. LaRouche is reported to have been subjected to harassment, investigation and prosecution solely because of his beliefs," the Special Rapporteur informed the assembled governments and delegates. Mr. D'Almeida Ribeiro "nevertheless felt obliged to ask the government of the United States of America to provide him with comments and observation thereon, since the allegations have been submitted to him with specific reference to the Declaration."

Then-Vice President Dan Quayle, who appeared before the U.N. Human Rights Commission February 10, 1992, did not comment, despite the serious nature of the charges, which include the fact that Mr. LaRouche is serving a death sentence due solely to his political beliefs. The U.S. government has declined to respond otherwise. Quayle did chose to lecture the assembled delegates about human rights violations by other nations, while ignoring charges against the United States itself.

The Special Rapporteur had taken up the case following the call of the International Progress Organization (IPO), delivered orally by Mr. Warren Hamerman on February 28, 1991, at the 47th annual plenary session.

The Special Rapporteur's 180-page report catalogued major human rights violations from 25 nations, which, he reported to the assemblage, had been compiled from "credible and reliable information coming before him and his work has been carried out with discretion and independence."

The text of the Special Rapporteur's citation reads as follows:

"The Special Rapporteur was not able to establish beyond doubt, whether Mr. LaRouche's association can be considered as falling under the terms of the Declaration on the Elimination of All Forms of Intolerance and of Discrimination Based on Religion or Belief. He nevertheless felt obliged to ask the government of the United States of America to provide him with comments and observations thereon, since the allegations have been submitted to him with specific reference to the Declaration.

"According to information received, United States citizen Mr. Lyndon H. LaRouche is reported to have been subjected to harassment, investigation and prosecution solely because of his beliefs. Mr. LaRouche, who is said to be founder and leader of a metaphysical association, whose beliefs are reportedly centered on the rights of all peoples to development and economic justice, was indicted 14 October 1988 and charged with 'conspiracy to commit fraud', 'mail fraud' and 'conspiracy to defraud the Internal Revenue Service.' On 27 January 1989, he was reportedly sentenced to 5 years imprisonment on each charge, amounting to a sentence of 15 years in prison, by the U.S. District Court of the Eastern District of Virginia, in Alexandria, Virginia. Mr. LaRouche's trial is said to have been unfair and conducted in disregard for guarantees necessary for the defense. Exclusion of evidence has also been reported in this connection as well as passing of excessive sentences for crimes which are usually said to be regarded as minor civil or administrative infractions. On 26 January 1990, Mr. LaRouche's appeal of sentence was denied by the Fourth Circuit Court of Appeals which upheld the sentence of the District Court of Alexandria. It has been alleged that about 50 persons have so far been indicted because of their links with Mr. LaRouche's association, and it has been reported that they, too, have had unfair trials.

"According to sources, Mr. LaRouche's beliefs have reportedly also resulted in seizure and closing down of 5 publishing companies whose publications have disseminated the ideas of his association." (Document E/CN.4/1992/52, p. 88, para. 74.)

IPO Calls on U.N. to Investigate U.S. Violations of Rights in LaRouche Case

Warren Hamerman of the International Progress Organization spoke at the United Nations Human Rights Commission plenary in Geneva, Switzerland on February 10, 1992, after a session that featured a speech by then-U.S. Vice President Dan Quayle, in which he boasted of America's triumph in the Gulf war against Iraq, and, among other things, stated, "The United States will, of course, always respect the sovereignty of nations. However, you should be forewarned: We shall not hesitate to speak the truth about clear violations of civil rights and civil liberties wherever they may be found, and whoever may be responsible. The days when a government charged with human rights abuses could cite 'sovereignty' or 'non-interference in internal affairs' as a defense, are gone. Today, whether we like it or not, we have all become our brother's keeper—not merely for our brother's sake, but for our own."

The United States declined to exercise its right to reply to the Hamerman speech, the text of which follows:

Presentation to the U.N. Human Rights Commission Plenary Session February, 1992 United Nations, Geneva

Agenda item: Implementation of the Declaration on the Elimination of All Forms of Discrimination Based on Religion or Belief

The Government of the United States has been asked by the Special Rapporteur to provide its comments to the charges that it is persecuting a man and his association solely for their beliefs in violation of the Declaration on the Elimination of All Forms of Discrimination Based on Religion or Belief.

The case is remarkable in the magnitude and nature of the human rights violation itself, despite the well-known guarantees *de jure* of freedom of expression for beliefs in the United States.

One year ago the gross human rights violations in the case of the American political prisoner Lyndon H. LaRouche, Jr. and his association were raised for the first time before the Human Rights Commission plenary session. It was presented again last August during the meeting of the Sub-commission in the context of an over-all disturbing pattern of systematic and widespread human rights violations in the United States.

Now the Government of the United States has been asked to reply to allegations about its actions in this human rights case by the Special Rapporteur, Mr. Angelo Vidal D'Almeida Ribeiro. The Special Rapporteur, after studying the documentation in the case, some months ago asked the Government of the United States of America to provide him with "comments and observations" on the allegations that in the LaRouche case it was in violation of the Declaration.

On page 88 of his report [E/CN.4/1992/52] to this session of the Human Rights Commission, the Special Rapporteur summarized the serious situation. . . .

As of this hour, the U.S. government has remained silent on these grave allegations, a tactic of non-recognition of human rights complaints which it has loudly condemned in other nations.

Given the special role it has sought as a kind of chairman of its vision of a "pax universalis," it is incumbent upon the U.S. Government to be held to the highest standards.

The United States has come frequently to the United Nations, including this morning the Vice President, to strongly condemn smaller nations for alleged human rights violations. In well-known instances the U.S. has even sought sanctions and gone to war against nations of the South in the name of righting these injustices.

Lest the appearance of double standards operate when the U.S. is the accused rather than the accuser, we urge the Commission to insist upon a full and impartial investigation or Enquête into these allegations.

From the standpoint of international law, the protection of human rights cannot be considered anymore as something that exclusively belongs to the State's internal affairs. As was rightly stated by several delegations at the 3,046th meeting of the Security Council on 31 January in New York (Security Council document S/23500), a policy of double standards in regard to the application of international legal principles would undermine the validity of those very principles.

The most fundamental questions of life and liberty are at stake here. LaRouche, currently living his 70th year, has just passed the third year of his imprisonment and is serving an effective death sentence for his beliefs, with no prospect for freedom within the average human life span.

In the new strategic world since the Gulf war and

collapse of the Soviet Union, the U.S. has now taken on the unchecked strategic role of defining before the United Nations its vision of justice and world order.

The International Progress Organization does not endorse the philosophic or political beliefs of Mr. LaRouche, yet we feel that the persecution of him and his followers by the government for their beliefs is a violation of fundamental human rights.

LaRouche was targetted for his political and philosophic beliefs just as others have been persecuted for their religious beliefs in cases where nations have gone outside international standards of civilized practice and law in order to suppress ideas and beliefs they viewed as threatening. Those beliefs can be briefly summarized in the following few themes.

Mr. LaRouche believes that the world is in an unprecedented crisis which threatens the existence of the entire human species. This crisis is economic, strategic, cultural, moral and spiritual in character. He believes that man has the capacity, in the living image of God, to create solutions to that crisis through using his creative powers of reason to make discoveries in science, and a new Renaissance in the classical arts, which can be translated into technological benefits, economic justice and an upgraded standard of living for all mankind, especially the poor. His beliefs strongly oppose all forms of demographic warfare against developing sector nations, debt-collection at the expense of human existence and all infringements against national sovereignty.

In these regards, his beliefs have strongly clashed with the prevailing policy commitments of the U.S. Government since the assassination of President John Fitzgerald Kennedy.

It is essential that the Human Rights Commission look with even sharper eyes and act with even greater resolution, given the fact that abuses are occurring in the very nation which has long been the justified world model for guarantees of free expression of beliefs, and ought to be restored to that standard again lest mankind's beacon of liberty be extinguished.

This is a test case. The concept of a New World Order is only meaningful if the basic principles of individual human rights can be enforced just as meaningfully for a citizen of a small nation as well as for a citizen from a global superpower. . . .

IPO President, Zepp-LaRouche Address U.N. Human Rights Commission

On August 19, 1992 in Geneva, Switzerland, Dr. Hans Koechler, president of the Vienna, Austria-based International Progress Organization, and Helga Zepp-LaRouche, wife of the jailed American political figure Lyndon H. LaRouche, addressed the session in Geneva of the United Nations Human Rights Commission, Sub-Commission on Prevention of Discrimination and Protection of Minorities.

United Nations Commission on Human Rights Sub-Commission on Prevention of Discrimination and Protection of Minorities

Forty-fourth session, Geneva, August 19, 1992

Agenda item 10: The administation of justice and the human rights of detainees

Agenda item 11: Independence and impartiality of the judiciary, jurors and assessors and the independence of lawyers

Presentation by Dr. Hans Koechler, president, International Progress Organization

Mr. Chairman,

When the International Progress Organization warned of serious abuses in the judicial system in the United States of America (see intervention by the IPO at the 43rd session of the Sub-Commission on Prevention of Discrimination and Protection of Minorities, 21 August 1991), it did so in the earnest hope, that steps would be taken to promptly remedy these abuses. A year has now gone by, and one must unfortunately conclude that not only have no remedial steps been taken, but developments show that the warnings uttered by the International Progress Organization must be reiterated today.

Without repeating in detail our remarks from a year ago, three aspects deserve to be mentioned in particular:

1. The practice of the **death penalty** in the United States. So far this year, 22 persons have been executed, more than in any other year since the death penalty was re-introduced to the United States in 1976. The turning point for world public opinion was the case of Roger K. Coleman, who was almost certainly innocent. A hearing to examine new evidence was denied, on the formal grounds that his defense had filed the motion one day late. In spite of appeals by the Pope, by high officials of nations closely allied to the United States, by thousands of individuals and civil rights organizations, Coleman was executed on May 20th, 1992.

Flying in the face of the international outcry, the death penalty continues to be carried out. The International Progress Organization takes this opportunity to support the European Parliament's resolution of June 11,

1992, most especially the appeal to candidates for high office in the United States to set an example by opposing the death penalty.

2. On 15 June 1992, the U.S. Supreme Court ruled that **kidnapping foreign citizens** abroad (*U.S. v. Alvarez-Machain*), to bring them to trial in the United States, does not contradict the U.S. Constitution. This decision by the Supreme Court under William Rehnquist, a decision strongly criticized by the minority of the Court, seeks to place U.S. law above all principles of international law. Both the Mexican and Canadian governments intervened as *amici curiae* against the U.S. in this instance, and a storm of protest broke out in Latin America when the decision was announced. Were this and other, similar decisions to be allowed to stand, we may expect a complete breakdown of the rule of law in the relations among nations.

3. The case of U.S. political prisoner Lyndon H. LaRouche, which the International Progress Organization has repeatedly brought to the attention of this body and the United Nations Commission on Human Rights, is of great concern to a growing circle of international observers.

The International Progress Organization today wishes to give the opportunity to the wife of Mr. Lyndon LaRouche, Mrs. Helga Zepp-LaRouche, to testify on human rights violations in her husband's case. With your permission, Mr. Chairman, I therefore will give the rest of my speaking time to Mrs. Helga Zepp-LaRouche.

Testimony by Helga Zepp-LaRouche

Mr. Chairman,
For more than three years and eight months my

husband, Lyndon LaRouche, presently an independent presidential candidate in the United States, has been jailed, though innocent, in an American prison in Rochester, Minnesota.

In a railroad trial, which trampled on all principles of the rule of law of a civilized nation, my husband was falsely charged and in reality condemned as a political dissident against the currently ruling American establishment, to fifteen years in prison. With him, the intent was to sink the political movement inspired by him. Yet, despite the banning—through a federally ordered bankruptcy ruling—of a scientific magazine spreading LaRouche's ideas, of a publishing company and of a weekly newspaper, as well as criminal proceedings against 50 further collaborators of my husband (with sentences of up to 77 years), the American prosecution authorities have not succeeded in wiping out this political movement.

Nonetheless, my husband, innocent, remains in prison, because massive injustice was committed in the trial. All appeals have upheld the verdict of Judge Albert V. Bryan. The same Judge Bryan (on May 18, 1992) rejected the last legal recourse, a motion for a new trial, and confirmed his own unjust verdict. The defense, under former U.S. Attorney General Ramsey Clark, documented the massive trial illegalities in 16 single points backed up by 6 massive files of evidence—none of which was seriously taken into consideration by Judge Bryan. One leading obstacle to a fair trial for my husband is the refusal on the part of President Bush and the prosecution, to release any exculpatory material, under the pretext of "national security reasons."

I have known my husband for over 20 years, and

have been happily married to him for 14 years, and I must say that I find him the most noble and selfless person I have ever met. He has devoted all his energies and his life's work to bring about a just new world economic order, which is in cohesion with the divine order of creation and which can guarantee the inalienable and human rights of each person living on this planet.

Indelibly printed in my memory is the impression left on me by our two discussions with Indira Gandhi regarding a 40-year development plan for India, designed by my husband, which she wanted to implement, before she was assassinated shortly after. In 1982 President Ló-pez Portillo of Mexico began to implement a program designed by my husband with the name of "Operation Juárez," which could have turned the Ibero-American continent into a prospering part of the world. From these and many other similar experiences over the last two decades, I know that literally millions of people look to my husband and his fight for a global reconstruction plan as the only hope and alternative to a worldwide Thirty Years' War, famine and depopulation. The same is true for the reemerging civil rights movement in the United States, which sees in my husband the person who is taking up the fight of Dr. Martin Luther King, at a moment when civil and human rights in the United States are trampled upon as never before.

These are the real reasons why, on orders of Dr. Kissinger among others, an unimaginable array of lies has been fabricated by the prosecution.

I still have the noise of the low-flying helicopters in my ears, which in the early dawn of October 6, 1986, buzzed our residence in Leesburg, while an armed "combat force" comprised of 400 military and police agents was deployed to raid our home, during which my husband, and possibly myself, were to be shot by storming agents. It was only a telegram to President Reagan and a worldwide mobilization which prevented a bloodbath. Documents today confirm the existence of this plan. The same documents confirm the suspicion I had at the time, that special units of the American military participated in the action and that the Pentagon collaborated fully in the operation! What a monstrous event, that the military should be deployed against a political opposition movement in the United States!

In my own activity as President of the Schiller Institute, I have had to experience time and again, how the same slanders and lies, spread in the judicial apparatus and "anti-LaRouche task force" against my husband, have also been retailed through American outfits, embassies and other international American organizations, against my work in Germany and that of my institute worldwide. Hundreds of documents, which have come into my hands through the FOIA (Freedom of Information Act), prove this to be the case.

I know that my husband is innocent. I, too, have personally experienced the machinations of his enemies in their attempt to "eliminate" him. Up until the present, the American judicial apparatus has obsequiously ratified an act of injustice which cries out to heaven for redress.

Next month my husband will have to spend his seventieth birthday behind prison walls. I appeal to you to do everything in your power, to liberate my innocent, jailed husband, and to render him justice, who has taken the cross for the millions, who are poor and have no voice in this world.

IPO Refutes U.S. Misrepresentation of LaRouche Case to U.N. Commission

On February 17, 1993, the International Progress Organization (IPO) again presented the case of Lyndon LaRouche to the ongoing 49th plenary session of the United Nations Human Rights Commission in Geneva. After the Special Rapporteur on Elimination of All Forms of Discrimination Based on Religion or Belief had included the LaRouche case into his report last year, the U.S. government sent a reply on March 24, 1992. The IPO intervened with corrections and comments to the U.S. government's reply. The IPO presentation by Ortrun Cramer follows.

Commission on Human Rights, 49th Session

Agenda Item 22: Implementation of the Declaration on the Elimination of All Forms of Intolerance and of Discrimination Based on Religion or Belief

Mr. Chairman,

On 8 November 1991 the Special Rapporteur monitoring violations of Intolerance and Discrimination Based on Religion or Belief formally transferred allegations of major human rights violations against Lyndon LaRouche and his associates to the United States Government. The Special Rapporteur's allegations against the United States were published in United Nations Document E/CN.4/1992/52, para. 74, dated 18 December 1991.

On 24 March 1992, the Government of the United States sent a reply to the Special Rapporteur containing numerous explicit misrepresentations of fact, distortions and obfuscations. The U.S. Government Reply is published in the February, 1993 Report of the Special Rapporteur to the Human Rights Commission (Document E/CN.4/1993/62).

The following specific examples illustrate the pattern:

1. The U.S. Government reply states that Mr. LaRouche "has been given due process under the laws of the United States," without making any mention of the fact that over two months before it submitted its reply, on January 22, 1992, the internationally known human rights advocate and former U.S. Attorney General Ramsey Clark, and other attorneys filed before a federal court six volumes of evidence newly discovered after trial that LaRouche was not afforded due process. The evidence was part of a more than 100-page *habeas corpus* motion, unprecedented in scope, which sought to vacate Mr. LaRouche's sentence because his conviction and detention were unlawful, based upon outrageous government misconduct. Massive evidence was presented by Ramsey Clark, et al. of at least nine provable major violations of due process. Mr. LaRouche was not present at any legal event where his *habeas* petition was being determined. The principal ground for LaRouche's demand for immediate release was that massive amounts of newly obtained evidence proved that "the prosecution conducted and participated in a conspiracy and concerted action with others to illegally and wrongfully convict him and his associates by engaging in outrageous misconduct, including financial warfare." This motion is currently on appeal before the Fourth Circuit Court of Appeals.

2. The U.S. Government reply is incorrect when

it states that the Alexandria convictions resulted from fraudulent fund-raising activities conducted by Mr. LaRouche and his supporters to finance his presidential campaigns. This is not true. None of the specific counts in the indictment against LaRouche or his associates involved funds to finance his presidential campaigns. Furthermore, at the sentencing hearing after trial the Court found that the total value of all transactions at issue was less than $300,000 and this money did not involve financing presidential campaigns.

3. The U.S. Government reply is incorrect when it states that some lenders lost their life savings. At the trial the U.S. Government presented perjured testimony from one lender witness, Elizabeth Sexton, whom they argued had lost her last dime to the LaRouche association. Subsequent to trial Mr. LaRouche's defense team obtained concrete documentation including bank and real estate records which showed that this woman had considerable financial means at the time and after the trial.

4. The U.S. Government reply asserts that a number of state authorities have investigated or prosecuted him and his associates for income tax crimes. There has not been a single state indictment or prosecution for income tax crimes.

5. The U.S. Government reply reports that Mr. LaRouche's Boston trial ended in a mistrial. They fail to report that the day after the mistrial a member of the jury stated publicly that the jury would have voted for acquittals because they believed that it was government targetting and misconduct which had caused the situation. Furthermore, they fail to inform the Special Rapporteur that the federal judge on the case, Robert E. Keeton, formally cited the government's "systemic and institutional prosecutorial misconduct." The government's prosecutorial team had steadfastly denied any and all entanglements which they had with private citizens and intelligence community "secret government" political enemies of LaRouche; they also denied the existence of any and all exculpatory evidence in this regard.

6. The U.S. Government feels obliged to state that Mr. LaRouche, though incarcerated, is continuing his political activities. This appears rather to be a line of defense against the growing wave of international protests the incarceration of Mr. LaRouche has prompted. The above-mentioned *habeas corpus* motion by Ramsey Clark and other attorneys concludes its extensive documentation: "This entire prosecution, and those actions preceding and succeeding it, were so corrupted by politically motivated misconduct and bad faith as to have overwhelmed any pretext of due process and fairness in the trial. . . . Relevant and exculpatory materials were intentionally and routinely withheld by the Government in an effort to preclude defenses, prevent discovery of the truth, and cover up the conspiracy and concerted action in which the Government was engaged."

The International Progress Organization also wants to draw the attention of the Commission to the testimony of Lyndon LaRouche's wife, Helga Zepp-LaRouche, to the Subcommission on the Prevention of Discrimination and Protection of Minorities of 19 August 1992, a summary of which is included in document E/CN.4/Sub.2/1992 SR.22. Mrs. LaRouche then stated: "One leading obstacle to a fair trial for my husband is the refusal on the part of President Bush and the prosecution, to release any exculpatory material, under the pretext of 'national security reasons.' "

Recently, well above 1,000 prominent personalities from around the world have appealed to incoming U.S. President Bill Clinton to break with the policies of his predecessor and free political prisoner Lyndon LaRouche. Among those who signed the appeal were a former head of state, parliamentarians, senators and former government officials from 16 countries; human rights activists and well-known representatives of civil rights movements, both from eastern Europe and from the United States; representatives from churches from around the world, artists, scientists, and newspaper publishers. The president of the International Progress Organization has endorsed this call to President Clinton.

Finally, the U.S. Government reply argues that LaRouche and his associates had ample opportunity to defend their rights in court up through the level of the U.S. Supreme Court. The International Progress Organization has in several presentations to this body and to the subcommission expressed its deep concern, shared by many in the field of international law, over the general collapse of judicial standards in the United States. . . .

The arrogant misrepresentations of the U.S. Government in its reply to the Special Rapporteur on the LaRouche case bespeaks a power which would substitute its own expediency for the principles of international law. We appeal to the Human Rights Commission to see to it that the United States Government, no matter how supreme its own self-conception as the sole remaining super-power on earth, must be held accountable to the same universal principles of international justice, human rights, and natural law as other civilized nations.

LaRouche Case Brought Before Organization of American States

Open Letter to the OAS, December 1992

The following open letter petitioning the Organization of American States on behalf of the imprisoned Lyndon LaRouche, was issued by the Commission to Investigate Human Rights Violations upon the occasion of the OAS meeting held December 14-15, 1992. It was signed by numerous Ibero-American political leaders, as well as persons from throughout the world.

To Ambassador Joao Baena Soares,
Secretary General:
To the participants at the Extraordinary Meeting of the OAS:

The Extraordinary Meeting of the Organization of American States will be considering possible changes to the OAS Charter, to automatically suspend from the regional organization any country in which democracy is interrupted or where grave violations of human rights are committed. Some are so concerned with defending democracy, that there is even talk of establishing mechanisms for collective military intervention in the country where the undesirable behavior occurs.

The undersigned, firm defenders of the inalienable rights of man, are wholly against the use of those rights, as a pretext to sneak the spurious concept of "limited sovereignty" into the OAS Charter and Inter-American relations. It is particularly worrisome that the strongest country in the Americas, wants to use the alleged defense of democracy and human rights as a pretext to turn Ibero-America into a protectorate, an integral component of the "new world order" proclaimed by George Bush on the eve of going to war against Iraq. More so, because the United States has promulgated the so-called Thornburgh Doctrine and the Torricelli Law, which violate the principles of international law, especially those pertaining to the sovereignty of nations.

Our suspicions about the true motives of the United States in raising the flag of human rights, are strengthened when we see the hypocrisy of Washington, a government that to this date has held economist and statesman Lyndon LaRouche captive after almost four years in prison. If the United States wants to discuss human rights, why don't they begin by clearing up this sordid case of political persecution?

Lyndon LaRouche, who for more than two decades has distinguished himself by defending the sovereign right of all nations—especially poor nations—to economic development, is the victim of a number of outrageous abuses that were carried out to silence him, to proscribe his ideas and to destroy his political movement. The trial that led to his imprisonment and that of several of his collaborators, was plagued with illegalities and irregularities, which have been publicly denounced by hundreds of jurists of the United States and many other countries, among them several judges and a former Attorney General. His case was presented to the United Nations Human Rights Commission in Geneva, which has requested the Government of the United States to provide a satisfactory explanation, so far to no avail.

This past Feb. 25, a delegation of Ibero-American parliamentarians met in Washington with Ambassador Joao Baena Soares, Secretary General of the OAS, to discuss the case of Lyndon LaRouche. The parliamentarians formally presented to Ambassador Baena a copy of the petition that LaRouche and five of his collaborators had submitted in July of 1991 to the Inter-American Commission on Human Rights of the OAS. Ambassador Baena promised the parliamentarians that he would personally take up the matter with the Human Rights Commission, but to this date the regional body has not fulfilled its responsibilities.

We therefore publicly call on the OAS and all its member states for an in-depth investigation of the case of Lyndon LaRouche and to take the necessary steps to remedy the ongoing gross violations against his human rights.

2255 Motion Seeks to Overturn LaRouche's Conviction

In January 1992, former U.S. Attorney General Ramsey Clark and Odin Anderson, attorneys for Lyndon LaRouche, filed a habeas corpus *motion, known as a 2255/Rule 33 motion, in federal court in Alexandria, Virginia, seeking to overturn LaRouche's conviction. Also appealing were co-defendants Edward Spannaus and William Wertz. This motion included volumes of new evidence obtained since LaRouche's conviction in 1988. Although trial judge Albert V. Bryan, Jr. denied the 2255 motion, it has been appealed to the Fourth U.S. Circuit Court of Appeals.*

After the 2255 Motion was filed, a pamphlet was published by the Commission to Investigate Human Rights Violations, containing a statement entitled "Enough Is Enough!" that was signed by over 500 jurists, human rights activists, and political figures, including persons from such newly freed countries as Georgia, Russia, Czechoslovakia, and Hungary. The statement calls for the "immediate release of LaRouche from prison," because of the "violations of due process which appear to have occurred in this case."

Recently, on December 28, 1992, a new motion was filed before the Fourth Circuit Appeals Court, requesting that court to take Judicial Notice of Certain Non-Record Items. These items, while not part of the record in U.S. v. LaRouche, et al., are exculpatory. These items came to light from the case U.S. v. Smith, et al. In the Motion printed below, references to other documents not part of this Motion are omitted.

Appellants' Motion Requesting That This Court Take Judicial Notice of Certain Non-Record Items

On December 16, 1992, this Court struck certain non-record items from the joint appendix of this appeal "without prejudice to the right of appellants to file a motion requesting that this Court take judicial notice of certain non-record items and appellants may accompany such a motion with a proposed attachment to their brief containing the items which appellants wish this Court to take judicial notice." By this motion, filed in accordance with the aforementioned Order, the appellants request that this Court take judicial notice of certain non-record items.

The subject of judicial notice is governed by Rule 201 of the Federal Rules of Evidence. Under F.R.E. Rule 201(d), a court "shall take judicial notice if requested by a party and supplied with the necessary information." F.R.E. Rule 201(f) empowers the federal courts to take judicial notice of facts outside the record "at any stage of the proceeding." This power allows appellate courts to take notice of factual developments which arise after the taking of an appeal. *Colonial Penn Ins. Co. v. Coil,* 887 F.2d 1236, 1239 (4th Cir., 1989).

Since the conclusion of the proceedings below, additional evidence relevant to this appeal has come to light. Much of this new evidence comes from the pending criminal trial, *U.S. v. Smith, et al.,* 92-420-A (E.D.Va.) The other sources of new evidence are the Government's own documents, released pursuant to the Freedom of Information Act, and a magazine article available to the general public. These latest revelations confirm the assertions made in the 2255/Rule 33 motion that the Government had engaged in a "continuing effort" (J.A. 50) to suppress exculpatory information and evidence and that appellants were continuing to obtain new and compelling evidence of this effort under the Freedom of Information Act and by other means.

The Kidnapping Case: *U.S. v. Smith, et al.*

In October 1992, the Government indicted Donald L. Moore, Edgar Newbold Smith, Galen Kelly, and others for conspiracy to kidnap and solicitation to kidnap. Mr. Moore, a former U.S. Deputy Marshal and Deputy Sheriff in Loudoun County, Virginia, figured prominently in the investigation and prosecution of these appellants. Besides Mr. Moore, the kidnapping case involves Galen Kelly, an acknowledged "deprogrammer," and Edgar Newbold Smith, the paterfamilias of a branch of the famous Du Pont family and financier of the kidnapping ring. The targets of the kidnapping plot, according to the indictment, were Lewis du Pont Smith and Andrea Diano Smith, the son and daughter-in-law of Edgar Newbold Smith.

In this case, the Government amassed evidence from consensually monitored tape recordings and court-ordered wiretaps of conversations involving Moore, Kelly, and Smith. Lurking behind this kidnapping ring is an organization known as the Cult Awareness Network (CAN), a national organization of "deprogrammers," which has been implicated in scores of kidnappings and related types of illegal conduct, and an organization dedicated to the destruction of the LaRouche movement. Moore, Kelly, and Smith are members of or associated with CAN. The case against these three individuals and their confederates continues to yield new evidence favorable to these appellants. Specifically, appellants are aware of new evidence relevant to the following issues raised in the appeal:

1. Bias of Trial Judge. There is evidence that the trial judge in this case, Albert V. Bryan, Jr., failed to disclose a communication he received from Edgar Newbold Smith which contained highly prejudicial information as well as a copy of an internal document from defendants' political organization. This undisclosed information powerfully supports the defendants' argument regarding the recusal of Judge Bryan. In their Brief, the appellants argued that the impartiality of Judge Bryan might reasonably be questioned and "that his view of the case may be influenced by extra-judicial considerations."

The surfacing of Edgar Newbold Smith's May 14, 1990 correspondence to Judge Bryan powerfully demonstrates this argument. On January 22, 1992, simultaneous with the filing of their 2255/Rule 33 motion, the appellants filed a motion to disqualify Judge Bryan. Without disclosing the Smith letter and its attachments, Judge Bryan denied this motion because the appellants failed to present evidence of extra-judicial bias. In fact, the judge was receiving extra-judicial information from a politically influential individual, Edgar Newbold Smith, a member of the prominent Du Pont family and relative of Pierre Du Pont, a 1988 candidate for the presidential nomination of the Republican Party. The judge's failure to disclose the Smith letter may reasonably be construed as an effort to conceal his bias.

The appellants request that this Court take judicial notice of the fact that Edgar Newbold Smith wrote and sent this letter to Judge Bryan and that Judge Bryan failed to disclose same letter to the appellants.

2. Deprogramming of Christian Curtis. The appellants request that this Court take judicial notice of the fact that there is evidence that a major Government witness at the defendants' trial, Christian Curtis, was "deprogrammed" and that Donald Moore knew Curtis had been deprogrammed. One published opinion involving Moore's alleged co-conspirator, Galen Kelly, described deprogramming as follows:

"The deprogramming process begins with abduction. Often strong men muscle the subject into a car and take him to a place where he is cut off from everyone but his captors. He may be held against his will for upwards of three weeks. Frequently, however, the initial deprogramming only lasts a few days. The subject's sleep is limited, and he is told that he will not be released until his beliefs meet his captors' approval." *Colombrito v. Kelly,* 764 F.2d 122, 125, n. 1 (quoting LeMoult, "Deprogramming Members of Religious Sects," 46 *Fordham L.Rev.* 599, 603-04).

The appellants' pretrial Brady requests sought information regarding the "psychiatric, physical, and/or mental examinations or histories of any Government witness," a request which covered hypnotism and other mind-altering techniques (J.A. 519-520). Since at least 1968, per *U.S. v. Miller,* 411 F.2d 825 (2nd Cir., 1968), prosecutors have been obliged to furnish the defense with evidence regarding the hypnosis of prosecution witnesses. Deprogramming, like hypnosis, is a mind-altering technique which may affect the jury's assessment of the weight and credibility of a witness's testimony. Under *Brady v. Maryland,* 373 U.S. 83 (1963) and progeny cases, the evidence of Curtis's deprogramming should have been delivered to the defense. Mr. Moore's revelation of the deprogramming of Christian Curtis provides further support for the appellants' argument that the Government committed multiple Brady violations with regard to Mr. Curtis. Mr. Curtis received immunity from the State of California and committed perjury on this issue at the appellants' trial. Mr. Curtis also received undisclosed rewards from government officials. Donald Moore knew of and participated in these blatant violations of the Brady rule.

3. Disruptive Activities Directed Against the

Finances of the Appellants. There is new evidence that Galen Kelly and Donald Moore participated in kidnapping activities against the LaRouche movement during the time period relevant to the appellants' indictment. There is evidence that shows Edgar Newbold Smith and Donald Moore discussed a policy of creating "a diminution of money flowing to" appellants' political movement. Moore repeatedly refers to this type of scenario as "busting the covey" and says that it is done "under the auspices of CAN."

In the 2255/Rule 33 motion, the appellants presented evidence that the Loudoun County Sheriff's Office worked with political opponents of the appellants "in coordinated activity designed to disrupt the financial activities of the [appellants'] political movement." The newly discovered evidence confirms this allegation. Donald Moore and Edgar Newbold Smith specifically discuss ways to diminish the flow of income to this movement. This is a precise example of the type of financial warfare which was designed and practiced against the appellants and their political movement, and which was the basis of their defense at trial and the focus of the evidence presented in their 2255/Rule 33 motion.

4. Conspiracy between Government Officials and Private Enemies of LaRouche. The Opinion of the District Court, denying the 2255/Rule 33 motion, charged the appellants with attempting "to erect a conspiracy out of mere policy disagreements with their opponents." J.A. 2315. The evidence in the public file of *U.S. v. Smith, et al.* contradicts the District Court and further substantiates appellants' argument that such a conspiracy existed and was not merely a matter of policy disagreements with political adversaries. There are admissions from Donald Moore that he has worked with Galen Kelly and Edgar Newbold Smith since 1985, the beginning of Moore's involvement in the LaRouche investigation. There are admissions from Donald Moore that he works for the Cult Awareness Network. There is evidence that Edgar Newbold Smith is a financial contributor to CAN. CAN is a political adversary which "works against" the appellants.

The evidence already revealed in the case of Donald Moore, Edgar Newbold Smith, and Galen Kelly manifestly supports the basic defense theory presented in pretrial motions. The appellants' defense at trial was that the Government, in concert with private enemies of the LaRouche movement, engaged in activities which impaired the defendants' ability to repay loans. The appellants' pretrial discovery and Brady requests sought evidence material to this defense. The Government denied the existence of such evidence. The truth now emerges that a principal member of the prosecution team in this case was, in concert with private enemies of the LaRouche movement, involved in kidnappings, deprogrammings, and activities designed to cause the "diminution of money flowing" to defendants' political movement. These are among the very issues raised by this appeal.

. . .

Additionally, at trial and in the 2255/Rule 33 motion, the appellants sought to establish a conspiracy and concert of action designed to defeat their political movement. The trial judge, after trial and in his denial of the 2255/Rule 33 motion, claimed this was "errant nonsense." Surely, the new evidence demonstrating the elaborate efforts of a notorious foreign spy service debunks the trial judge's prejudiced views and adds further weight to the arguments advanced by the appellants in their appeal.

Discussion

The normal rule that appellate courts may only review matters put before the district court "is subject to the right of an appellate court to take judicial notice of new developments not considered by the lower court." In *Landy v. F.D.I.C.*, 486 F.2d 139 (3rd Cir., 1973). Per F.R.E. 201(f), appellate courts are "free to take judicial notice of subsequent developments in cases that are a matter of public record and are relevant to the appeal." *Rothenberg v. Security Management Co.*, 667 F.2d 958, 961 (11th Cir., 1982); *see also, Parrish v. U.S.*, 376 F.2d 601, 603 (4th Cir., 1967) (court takes judicial notice of subsequent events). In another Fourth Circuit case, *Colonial Penn Ins. Co. v. Coil*, supra, this Court took judicial notice, per F.R.E. 201, of a factual development occurring after the conclusion of the district court proceedings because this development was "relevant to a just and fair decision in this case." *Colonial Penn Ins. Co. v. Coil*, 887 F.2d at 1239. For similar reasons, this court should take judicial notice of the facts described below and attached in documentary form to this motion.

F.R.E. Rule 201(b) specifies that judicially noticed facts must be ones that are "not subject to reasonable dispute" because they are either generally known or otherwise "capable of accurate and ready determination by resort to sources whose accuracy cannot reasonably be questioned." Every fact, except one, offered for judicial notice is derived from the United States Government, either in the form of court records from the Smith case or from FBI documents released under the Freedom of Information Act.

The Government cannot reasonably dispute, for example, that tape recordings and transcripts exist in the court file of *U.S. v. Smith, et al.* memorializing conversations where Donald Moore makes the statements attributed to him in the foregoing pages. The Government may wish to contest the accuracy of these statements, but this testing of Mr. Moore's veracity must await an evidentiary hearing. The threshold issue is whether the appellants are entitled to an evidentiary hearing and, for these purposes, the appellants' factual allegations must be taken as true.

For reasons previously stated, the appellants request that this Court take judicial notice of the following facts incorporated in non-record items:

1. In or about October 1992, the United States of America indicted Edgar Newbold Smith, Galen G. Kelly, Robert Point, and Donald L. Moore under 18 U.S.C. 1201 for conspiracy to kidnap Lewis du Pont Smith and Andrea Diano Smith, and also indicted Edgar Newbold Smith and Donald L. Moore under 18 U.S.C. 373 for solicitation to kidnap Lewis DuPont Smith and Andrea Diano Smith. Said case is captioned *U.S. v. Smith, et al.*, 92-420-A.

2. The court records in *U.S. v. Smith, et al.* contain a transcript of a consensually monitored conversation where Donald Moore states that he worked on the LaRouche case.

3. In the case of *U.S. v. Smith, et al.*, the court papers of the United States acknowledge that Edgar Newbold Smith is the father of Lewis du Pont Smith and the father-in-law of Andrea Diano Smith, and that Lewis du Pont Smith and Andrea Diano Smith are associates of appellant Lyndon LaRouche.

4. The court records in *U.S. v. Smith et al.* contain a letter written on or about May 14, 1990 by Edgar Newbold Smith and forwarded to Judge Albert V. Bryan, Jr. The appellants request that this Court take judicial notice of the contents of the letter and the fact that it was forwarded to Judge Albert V. Bryan, Jr.

5. Judge Albert V. Bryan, Jr. did not disclose the existence and contents of Edgar Newbold Smith's May 14, 1990 letter to the appellants during the course of the 2255/Rule 33 litigation or at any other time.

6. The court records in *U.S. v. Smith et al.* contain a transcript of a consensually monitored conversation wherein Donald L. Moore states that Christian Curtis, a witness at the trial of these appellants, had been "deprogrammed."

7. The court records in *U.S. v. Smith, et al.* contain a transcript of a consensually monitored conversation wherein Donald L. Moore states his awareness of Galen Kelly's efforts to kidnap Lewis du Pont Smith dating back six years.

8. The court records in *U.S. v. Smith, et al.* contain a transcript of a consensually monitored conversation wherein Edgar Newbold Smith and Donald L. Moore discuss a policy of creating "a diminution of money" flowing to appellants' political movement.

9. Donald Moore discussed scenarios for financially disrupting the appellants' political movement, generically referred to such scenarios as "busting the covey," and said "busting the covey" was done "under the auspices of" the Cult Awareness Network.

10. The court records in *U.S. v. Smith, et al.* contain transcripts of consensually monitored conversations wherein Donald L. Moore states he has worked with Galen Kelly and Edgar Newbold Smith since 1985, the beginning of Moore's involvement in the LaRouche investigation.

11. The court records in *U.S. v. Smith, et al.* contain transcripts of consensually monitored conversations wherein Donald L. Moore states that he works for the Cult Awareness Network.

12. The court records in *U.S. v. Smith, et al.* contain transcripts of consensually monitored conversations where Donald L. Moore and Edgar Newbold Smith state that Edgar Newbold Smith is a financial contributor to the Cult Awareness Network.

13. The court records in *U.S. v. Smith, et al.* contain a transcript of a consensually monitored conversation which shows that the Cult Awareness Network is an adversary of the appellants and works against them.

14. According to an FBI document in the custody of the New Haven Field Office, a person, whose name is redacted, signed a statement on October 10, 1986 reflecting a pre-existing agreement to voluntarily record phone conversations with representatives of Caucus Distributors, a company formerly associated with the appellants. The signer of the statement agreed to furnish these recorded phone conversations to the FBI. . . .

16. According to *Journalisten*, a former agent of the East German secret police (Stasi) stated that the Stasi orchestrated the false campaign alleging that the appellants were responsible for the assassination of Olof Palme.

The alternative to judicial notice of these matters is for the appellants to file a second 2255/Rule 33 motion to put evidence in the record which, but for the trial judge's denial of an evidentiary hearing, would have been revealed during the proceedings below. This approach forces the appellants to litigate for their freedom in a piecemeal fashion, which is to their detriment and to the detriment of sound judicial administration. The prospect of such a burdensome and time-consuming procedure is precisely why appellate courts recognize their power to take judicial notice of subsequent events as "consistent with the avoidance of piecemeal appeals." In Re Search Warrants (Executed on January 23, 1983), 750 F.2d 664, 668 (8th Cir., 1984). In the interests of judicial economy and to safeguard these appellants from the prejudice caused by the Government's persistent stonewalling on the production of Brady material, this Court should take judicial notice of the matters presented by the appellants. . . .

INDEX

249